BIBLICAL PSYCHOLOGY
3rd Edition

Thomas J. Edgington, Ph.D. and Linda K. Edgington

A textbook that explores what the Bible has to say about the thinking and behavior of man.

BIBLICAL PSYCHOLOGY
TABLE OF CONTENTS

PREFACE

As a psychology professor, I have examined numerous textbooks and miscellaneous writings through the years. I have found books by Christian psychologists that deal with psychological topics but don't give an in-depth theological discussion, as well as books by theologians that touch on psychological topics but often lack a thorough understanding of the field of psychology. Given my theological (M.Div.) and psychological (M.A. and Ph.D.) training, I wanted to tackle the subject of psychology from a theological vantage point in a way that I felt would be most helpful to myself and others. Though compiling the workbook, *Healing Helps from the Bible* [1] (that specifically addresses biblical references to psychological topics), I still felt something needed to be written for the Christian psychology professor and student that approached psychology from a theological basis and in a precise and easily understood manner. This work (and its companion work, *Theological Foundations of Counseling,*) has been compiled so that Christian teachers have a better format from which to teach the subject of psychology and students are able to learn the importance of studying the subject from a Christian and biblical perspective.

A second reason for writing this, along with *Theological Foundations of Counseling,* is my hope to dispel some of the misconceptions about psychology which have been "thrown around" in Christian circles. Some of this confusion has been perpetuated through the years by popular authors, speakers, and others in the Christian community who have rightly observed the lack of scriptural emphasis in counseling and/or observed people neglecting to use pastors for help. Those Christian observers took note of reliance on psychological techniques and assumptions that did not seem to be God-honoring or in line with Christian teachings. Many of those people were godly men and women who reacted and then made an attempt to "swing the pendulum" back to the importance of biblical training. In doing so, however, they may have gone too far at times -- leading many to over-generalize and consequently discount any importance of the subject of psychology at all. To many of these Christians, the teachings of some psychologists equaled "psychology." In my experience

---

[1] Thomas J. Edgington, *Healing Helps from the Bible* (Winona Lake, IN: Self-Published and printed through Evangel Press, 1995).

this overgeneralization seems to be an important aspect of the problem.

Some who misunderstand psychology base their conviction on the concept that all psychology is intending to affirm the entire teachings, findings, and conclusions of Freud, Skinner, and others who did not hold to Christian beliefs. Others' ideas can be summarized in the following misconceptions by Christians: 1) Psychology teaches people to "avoid taking responsibility and blame everything on their parents." 2) Psychology espouses the beliefs: "I am a victim" and "I am not responsible for my own sin." 3) Psychologists do not believe in discipline -- only a sort of "namby-pamby" dialogue which they employ to resolve conflict or disobedience.[2] 4) Psychology is geared to make people "feel good" and does not confront the sinner. 5) Psychological teachings instruct us to be "selfish" (an "I'm worth it" type of philosophy) in a way that looks after our own needs to the exclusion of others.

My hope is that as students study psychological principles in this textbook, they will learn that there is much that can be gleaned when looking at psychology (thinking and behavior) from a biblical perspective.

---

[2] Though calm discussion is appropriate when conflict arises and being "slow to become angry" is certainly biblical (James 1:19); there comes a time to act with strength and authority. "psychology" has often been linked to a type of "namby-pamby" pandering that reinforces selfish behavior. Though that is a "method" that has been employed by some psychologists, it is not something that defines "Psychology." The belief that that type of pandering discussion is the only way to resolve conflicts is certainly contradicted by Christ's own demonstration of anger toward the money changers and others buying and selling in the temple as noted in Matt. 21:12 & Mark 11:15. What authority He must have had to overturn tables and benches and "not allow anyone to carry merchandise through the temple courts."

INTRODUCTION

Why is there a need to talk about a biblical psychology? There are many misconceptions about the relationship between the Bible, theology, and psychology -- especially in the Christian world. Some feel that the words "Bible" and "psychology" should never be used together. The purpose of this book (and its companion book: *Theological Foundations of Counseling*) is to show that not only can they be used in the same phrase, but without an understanding of the Bible and theology, a proper sense of psychology cannot take place. We will look at this topic in depth in chapter 2, to show that the Bible and psychology can intersect in a way that is biblical.

The first chapter of this book will focus on **presuppositions**. Presuppositions are important because where we start will determine where we end.

In the second chapter, we will talk a little about **integration**. Though I don't like the term "integration" (I will explain why later), we will use it for our purposes in this chapter. We will raise the question of whether there are better ways of describing how the disciplines interrelate, rather than using the term "integration." A number of faulty "Christian" definitions of psychology will be mentioned. And we will consider how faulty definitions have prevented some from learning the truths of what God has given us through His word and further truths bestowed to others through the common grace of God.

Personality is an important topic for psychology. We will examine a proper definition of personality in chapter 3 and look at what the Bible has to say about personality as a reflection of the image of God.

Chapter 4 deals with the subject of **unconscious sin**. Some (like Freud) believe the unconscious forces are a part of our personality – even determining aspects of our personality. Is there such a realm in us? Does the Bible refer to an unconscious part of us? Can sin be unconscious? These questions will be explored.

Dreams are a fascination to many. Freud believed that dreams were the "royal road" to the unconscious. Are they? Did God design us to dream? If so, what is the purpose of dreams? The Bible gives us some data about dreams. We will look at some data from researchers as well.

Some may believe that the topic of **self-concept** or commonly referred to as "self-esteem," is not biblical and should not be discussed by Christians. Biblical dignity is something that God desires for all of us. It will be demonstrated in this book that the Bible does address the topic of our self-concept, indicating how we should view ourselves.

Bible versions used and quoted in this book are the New International Version (NIV), New American Standard Version (NASB), the King James Version (KJV), and the New Living Translation Version (NLV). If not given, it can be assumed that the quote is from the NIV.

CHAPTER 1
PRESUPPOSITIONS

Everyone believes in something. Even if we believe that there is nothing to believe in, that is a belief. We all build our thinking and live our lives according to those beliefs or set of assumptions. In order to develop a biblical psychology, we must start with a set of assumptions that will be termed "presuppositions."

1. Transcendence and Immanence
(There is Transcendence. There is Immanence.)

DEFINITIONS

As Christians we assume two important things: 1. We believe that there is another world outside of our own. 2. We believe that this world, our present world, is created. We believe in **Transcendence and Immanence**.

"Transcendence," in the strictest sense of the term, means that "non-created" world that "transcends" all time and creation. That could only include God.

"Immanence," in the strictest sense of the term, means "all that God created." This would include man, animals, earth, the universe, etc., along with heaven, angels, Satan (a fallen angel), spirits, etc. Typically however, most people and most theologians do not use these terms in their strictest senses.

The more common usage of the word "transcendence" refers to things that we *cannot* physically experience -- see, touch, hear, smell, or taste -- at this time. One designation is that the term "transcendence" denotes things that are "unseen" (broadly used to indicate things that are not physically experienced through man's five senses). *As typically used, **transcendence** includes God, along with Heaven, angels, Satan, spirits, demons, etc.*

When we think of "immanence," we tend to think more commonly about that which is "immanent" to us -- those things that we *can* see, touch, or physically "sense" in some way. *Immanence can be distinguished as those things which are "seen"* (or those things physically acknowledgeable by earthly man through his five senses) -- *including the earth, stars, man, animals, etc.* For the intent of this book, the more common reference to the terms "transcendence" and "immanence" will be used.

Whether the distinction is termed "Unseen vs. Seen" or "Transcendent vs. Immanent," as Christians we believe that a world exists that is outside of our current physical experience. God created a world that we can't see, a world we can't get to. We can't take a bus trip today to Heaven. We can't see it, yet we still believe that there is a vast, other world.

It is an accepted belief, a "presupposition," for us. We "presuppose" it to be true. We assume that God and Heaven exist, without a need to be convinced, because God and Heaven are part of our belief system. They are part of a world that is "unseen" for us.

THERE EXISTS ANOTHER WORLD

But are there people who don't believe in God, who also believe this presupposition -- that there is a world that we can't see? During the months following the terror attacks of September 11, 2001, photos[3] surfaced which observers claimed revealed spirits or "evil." Many were heard proclaiming verbally or in  emails that they could see the shape of "the devil," "a demon," "evil personified," in the images of smoke rising from the twin towers. The people were talking about evil. They were talking about something Satanic.

Many of those imaginings came from people who didn't even go to church. And though church was not a part of their lives, they were talking about demons and guardian angels -- supposing that there were angels

---

[3] Twin towers image -- public domain. January 5,2012, from
http://billieshelppageforpainunderstanding.org/911.htm.

there to help the distressed or deceased people. Pictures were created with angels superimposed who were holding, comforting, or directing victims of the attack. Those considering such things were not necessarily believers. Many certainly didn't follow a conservative theology.

I was once invited into the office of a clinician and noticed crystals hanging up on the window. So I asked the clinician, "What are those?

She responded, "Oh, those crystals give me power."

Becoming even more curious, I asked her to tell me more. She explained that there was energy in the crystals. Sometimes she would stare at them. Sometimes she would rub them. Sometimes she had clients also do those same things. The crystals would then empower her or empower her clients, she said.

She had put her belief in crystals. She presupposed that they had an energy that was important to acquire.

Our presuppositions will affect who we are. If there is another world other than our own, would you say that has huge implications on who we are and how we behave?

And if you say, "This world is it. This is all there is. We are here simply by time and chance -- evolutionary forces"; that presupposition is HUGE! Because if "this is it," how are we going to think and behave?

"Seize the day?"[4] Seek personal happiness? Learn to cope and adapt?

What about morality? Does morality make any sense? What type of person would one be?

What if we believe "there *is* another world"? -- proposed in Presupposition 1. And what if we believe "there *is* a God"? -- Presupposition 2 (which will be discussed in the next section). Just add those two: 1) another world and 2) God. How will that affect who we are? Does morality now make sense? A presupposition of a spiritual world (transcendent) has many implications.

One of the divisions in the American Psychological Association is "Spirituality." It is interesting that an organization that uses General Revelation as its base for knowledge would include a division that pertains

---

[4] Translated "Seize the day," from the Latin phrase, "Carpe Diem," used by the ancient philosopher and poet, Horace (65 BC - 8 BC), and popularized contemporarily by the 1986 movie, "Dead Poets Society."

to spirituality.

Why? Could it be that they know there is more? Ecclesiastes 3:11 says that God has "set eternity in the hearts of men."[5] We know there is more!

How many times have people said, "There's got to be more than this"? They're right. When we assume that there is another world out there -- a transcendent world, it will affect us psychologically.

2. There Exists a "Personal God"

Now, add the second assumption: There is a God, a PERSONAL (key word here) being, who is transcendent and who dwells in transcendence.

Genesis 1:1, "In the beginning *God* created . . ."

Where did He come from? How did he get there? Had He been planning? When did He start planning? How long did it take Him to plan?

These are things that children often ask their parents. "Where did God come from?" "How old is He?" "How could someone just always be?"

All the Bible says is, "In the beginning, GOD. . ." The Bible assumes His presence. It says that He is eternally present in the past. That's all we know. We just have to believe it.

Exodus 3:14, "I am who I am." What's He trying to say?

Moses: "Who should I say sent me?"

"Tell them, 'I am' sent you."

"What is your name?"

"I am that I am"

What is God trying to say? He is trying to say something about His name. His name is important. His name is trying to say, "I'm the self-sufficient one," "I'm it," "I'm what it's all about," ". . . I am." Christ

---

[5] Unless otherwise indicated all Bible references in this book are quoted from the New International Version.

came along and said, "I am the bread of life, I am the living water . . . I am."

Now here's the important part: **He's a personal being**. He's not a blob. He's not a "force" (like that referred to in the *Star Wars* movies -- "May the *force* be with you"). He is a PERSONAL being who is really out there.

And not only is He "out there," but He is everywhere -- omnipresent.

He is not IN everything; that would be Pantheism. But everything is within His grasp. He is omnipresent.

So right now God sees us and He can take hold of us if He needs to. That probably doesn't mean that He's flowing through the room necessarily, but He is saying, "I see you. I can take hold of you at any moment."

So what are the implications of this for us? If God is personal, what makes that different from being "the force"? How is that different from a God who is a "blob"? Or how is that different from a belief that there is just some "force of good and/or evil" out there?

Accountability could be a positive consequence of our belief in God. If God is personal, if He is a person, then we are accountable to someone.

That belief could also impact our thinking in negative ways. We could think, "Where was He? If He's personal and He loves me and He could have been there, why wasn't He?"

Now we could say, "Maybe He started all of this and then said, 'Now you guys do whatever you want and I'm going to be in heaven and whatever you do is up to you.'"

But, that's not what the Bible tells us. The Bible says we are accountable to Him. We are going to give an account. We are going to answer to Him.

Now think about it. If God created personal beings, it only makes sense that He would think, "I've invested something in you. I made you like me. I want to know that you're doing some things that I want you to do."

And IF we believe that we are personally accountable to a God and one day we will have to give an answer for how we lived our lives, does that change how we think and how we live our lives? Probably so.

GOD IS A GOOD GOD

This brings us to a sub-point: The person we are accountable to, is a GOOD God. So a sub-point to Presupposition number 2 is the presupposition that "God is good." -- "He's righteous."

We are accountable to someone who has our best interests in mind. That is different from a God who is a tyrant, a God who is like Zeus -- who is fickle and leaves us never knowing what is going to happen or what we can depend on. We have a God who is perfectly righteous. This is an important sub-point to our presupposition.

IMPLICATIONS

So the question then is: "What makes Christians different? What makes Christian Psychology different? Does it give us more hope? We would say so, but some people in the secular world say that they have hope. Does it make us more cautious? Yes, possibly, but some in the secular world are cautious. Does it make an internal difference? Yes, I believe so; but how? In what way?

The difference is our goals and the theology that we base those goals upon. Our theology drives what we do. Because of that theology, the goals of a Christian are very different from those of the secular world.

In the secular world, the goal is coping and adapting and looking for ways to be happy. But that is also kind of a "skyhook" -- "I want to be happy." And what are you grounding your happiness in? "Nothing, I just want to be happy."

But, what is interesting is that the existentialists will say, "That's the way it is, There is no ground." Their word is "groundlessness." There is no ultimate rock. There is no ultimate hope. There is nothing. The existentialist would say that you are out there on your own, BUT you are small "g" god and you can create meaning and purpose -- therefore, that's what life is all about.

If we don't have the first two presuppositions -- "There is another world" and "There is a personal God" -- then we are not going to be driven to know God better and to serve God because that wouldn't make any sense. There would be no transcendence. There would be no God. So personal happiness would be what life is all about. That is what would make sense.

But even Christians have said, "Isn't happiness what it's all about? Doesn't God want us to be happy?" Not necessarily.

It is clear that God likes happiness. The Bible demonstrates that in numerous places. It talks about having a happy/cheerful heart" in Proverbs 15:13 and 17:22. Psalms is filled with verses describing joy as a positive experience desired by God. David "danced before the Lord" (2 Sam. 6:14) -- an indication that this "man after God's own heart" enjoyed events in his life. In Luke 2:11, the shepherds were told by an angel, "I bring you good news of great joy. . ." God doesn't want us to be "overwhelmed by excessive sorrow" (2 Cor. 2:7). And ultimately, God wants us to be happy.

But in this present world, to be in some kind of constant "euphoric state" is not what God seems to have in mind. And sometimes, the best way to understand joy is to have something to compare it with -- pain.

Christ felt deep sadness and was known as a "Man of Sorrows" (Isa. 53:3); yet Paul talks about contentment in spite of his trials (Phil. 4:11). So something seems to be even more important than a perpetual state of happiness in response to our world and events in our lives, and that is godliness. True godliness will lead to contentment.

Contentment is a deeper form of happiness. Contentment says, "I'm okay, even if my circumstances aren't. I have hope, even when it seems hopeless. I have enough, even if it seems like there is not enough to go on."

We can actually use life's difficulties to find God. We can learn to know deeper peace when we go through trials and problems. But is that something that comes easily for a Christian?

Even Paul asked God not once, but THREE TIMES, to remove a particular "thorn in his flesh" (2 Cor. 12:9)! Yet what was God's answer? ". . . My power is made perfect in weakness." We can find God in a deeper way and display His grace with more power when we are confronted with life's difficulties.

Yet, some attempt to USE God to solve their problems. If we USE God to solve our problems, then who is God? When we try to manipulate God to give us what we want or to get us out of pain or to change a situation, who is trying to be in control? We are.

We sometimes approach God like He is a cosmic Santa Claus who will give us what we want whenever we ask for it, rather than saying, "Maybe God is allowing me to have this depression, or this anxiety, or this marital/family problem, or this sleep problem, or this illness, or whatever it is . . . Maybe He's allowing that, so that I can find Him in a new way." Many times it is when we have really struggled with life's difficulties that we are able to understand God in a new way. And maybe He also allows those we care about -- a friend or a child or a family member -- to have difficulty so that we all can know Him better as well.

So if that is true, how does that affect the way we think and respond to problems? We don't want to have struggles. We want to have "happy thoughts" and good circumstances. But maybe the ultimate goal is not for us to have all of our desires fulfilled. Maybe through difficult times, we are going to find God; and when that happens, we will actually enjoy our lives more! Maybe we will find God in a new, deeper way. We may know Him a little better. We may want to serve Him more.

Christians who unexpectedly find themselves struggling with depression have been known to change their approach to others. When asked, "Before you became depressed, what would you have told others who were depressed?" (This includes committed Christians); the answer is often, "You're not trusting God enough." "You need to read the Bible more." "Quit feeling sorry for yourself and get on with your life!" "Go out and help somebody! Your problem is selfishness and you need to quit thinking about yourself and go help someone else!"

Yet after battling through the same difficult situation -- maybe it was the loss of a child or a job or maybe it was a disease or cancer or rape, the response often changes to something like this: "I'd tell them, 'Let's talk. Can we talk?'"

Because of our pain, sometimes we become better "lovers." God uses our pain as a way of helping us to love people better. And pain often bonds us to others. We feel a connection; and it can also be an avenue of leading a fellow sufferer to Christ. God, in His infinite wisdom, knows what we need in order to enjoy life more -- and sometimes that is pain that appears to make no sense to us.

The poem on the next page by Bob Perks is written as a wish from a parent to a daughter. Maybe that is what good parents should wish for their children. Maybe that is what God desires for us.

ENOUGH

I wish you enough sun to keep your attitude bright.
I wish you enough rain to appreciate the sun more.
I wish you enough happiness to keep your spirit alive.
I wish you enough pain so that the smallest joys in life appear
much bigger.
I wish you enough gain to satisfy your wanting.
I wish you enough loss to appreciate all that you possess.
I wish you enough "Hellos" to get you through   the
final "Good-bye."[6]

Now, do we want to struggle or to see those we care about struggle? No! Not at all! But in the "pit," sometimes something can happen that is bigger than not being depressed or being healthy, or making lots of money, or being treated fairly all the time, etc., because the two greatest commandments are: "Love God with your heart, soul, and mind," and "Love your neighbor as yourself."

Through pain, we can learn how to love a neighbor better. We can even learn to love God more. We can appreciate His comfort, and His mercy, and His grace. Before loss, we often don't see the NEED for any of that.

So one may not feel the need to stay very close to God when comfortable and "having it all together." But, when someone is in the "pit" and when all that can be said is, "Help!" that is often when God does His greatest work. And sometimes maybe God wants us there because dependency is more important than feeling good and having immediate personal happiness.

Believing in a personal God causes us to focus on Him and His ultimate purpose. We realize we are dependent beings and when we struggle and have pain, we understand God is in control and wants to accomplish something in and/or through us. That dependency on God gives us a rock for our foundation, which provides us the strength and determination to carry on.

---

[6]Bob Perks, "I Wish You Enough," http://www.motivateus.com/stories/iwish2.htm, Copyright © 2001. Bob has also published a book with the same name -- *I Wish You Enough!* – published by Thomas Nelson Publishers, based on the "Eight Wishes" given in the poem. Permission to use poem granted by Bob Parks, 10/5/10.

3. Everything Reflects God

Presupposition number 3: "There is a God who is the creator and sustainer of everything; therefore, **everything reflects God**."

If you have ever created something -- drawn something, painted something, sculpted something, built something, decorated something, invented something -- you realize that your creation says something about you. If someone were to examine your product, what might that person learn about you? That person might learn that you are very detailed. He/she may learn that you take pride in what you do. Maybe the examiner would learn that you are a very bold person, that you have a sense of humor, or that you care about others. You can't create without your creation saying, "Here's me," because it is YOU coming out onto that piece of paper or in that building or whatever it is that you have created.

It is the same with God. When He created the world, the world said, "Here's God." It was telling us something about its creator. It was saying, "This is what God is like. This demonstrates something about God."

Everything in the world that God created, reflects God -- including us. We reflect God. We illustrate who He is.

So does it make sense to study psychology? If psychology is: "The study of mental and behavioral processes" and God created those mental and behavioral processes, does it make sense that we can get to know God better by studying His creation -- which involves those things?

This point is important because some Christian people have said that psychology is sinful, "of the devil," and shouldn't be studied. But, if psychology is something that God created (Psychology must be defined correctly -- as the study of our thinking and behavior -- because if one starts with a faulty definition of psychology, the result will be a faulty conclusion as to whether we should study it or not), then doesn't it make sense that studying it will help us know God better? (Psalm 111:2).

If God created psychology -- mental and behavioral processes, if that is true, does psychology reflect God? Would Biology reflect God? How about Philosophy? Mathematics?

How does math reflect God? There are laws that make sense. With math there is order; and importantly, with math comes an understanding of infinity.

Most of us remember some childhood experience that involved

infinity. The conversation probably went something like this: "I'm going to do this one hundred million zillion times" to which the friend responds, "I'm going to do it one hundred million zillion and one!" which is countered with, "I'm going to do it one hundred million zillion and two." And this could keep going on and on with each one trying to "better" the other's statement. There is no end to how far it could go. With math, we understand something about infinity.

Everything in the world, everything here, reflects God -- including us. So what are the implications for us to consider?

First of all, the whole idea of "Creation versus Evolution" comes to the forefront of our consideration. Could all of this have happened by chance, without some sort of plan or design?

But if God created everything, then it makes sense that we ought to know the creator and understand His design. And life works better if we take the time to know and understand our creator and His design for this world and for us.

A number of years ago when our children were small, I put together a swing set. As I unpacked the materials, I quickly set aside the paper that was included in the box with a list of steps on how it was to be assembled.

"Instructions?" I thought, "I'm a man; I don't need instructions. I can do this."

I laid it all out. "It's simple! It's a swing set. There's nothing hard about this!"

But I found it was a tedious job. There were lots of nuts and bolts and pieces to screw together.

When I got to the second-to-the-last step, I was ready to attach the swing to the rod that went through the hollow pole at the top. I looked at the ground and there was the rod! Everything else on the swing set was put together.

As I stared at the rod and then at the hollow pole, I came to a sobering realization, "Hmmm, that was probably supposed to be in there, so I could attach the swing to that." My heart sank.

Realizing I had made a mistake, I dismally began unscrewing the pieces. I ended up taking the WHOLE swing set apart, because when I looked at the instructions I noticed that it said, (in clear, bold letters) to make sure to put the rod in BEFORE proceeding. Needless to say, I was NOT a "happy camper."

After I got it all apart, I put the rod in, put the whole thing back together, and attached the swings. But what should have been a two-hour job turned out to be about a six-hour job. If I had just looked at the instructions first, I could have saved myself a lot of trouble!

Do you think maybe God is saying that? "If you would just take a look at how I created things and understand what I intended, it would make life go a lot better than your efforts to do it on your own."

The evolutionist says, "There is no God; therefore . . ." What? "Cope. Adapt. Find personal happiness. That's what it's all about." Maybe there is more.

The study of psychology reflects God. It is the same as biology, chemistry, physics, math, and philosophy; it all reflects God and it is all worth studying.

After learning about amoebas, a Christian college student was struck with their intricacy in her biology class. "I don't know how people cannot believe there is a God," she shared. "There are thousands of detailed characteristics to this one-celled creature. How do you not believe in God?"[7]

Yeah! Wow! Look what God did with amoebas! Compare that to the biggest star. Whoa! He is big God! It is pretty awesome to try to fathom what God is all about. And that reflection of God has huge implications for psychology!

4. God Has Revealed Himself to Us

Presupposition Number 4: Not only is God's creation a reflection of Him, but it is a revelation of Him as well. It doesn't just demonstrate to us what God is like, but it is also one way He communicates to us about Himself. In essence, God says, "I'm going to tell you about me." The following are five ways that God tells us about Himself.

---

[7] Comment made by relative of author.

GOD HAS REVEALED HIMSELF THROUGH NATURE

When you experience a storm or when you see anything -- the beauty of mountains or trees, God is being revealed. (This was discussed this in the previous section.) In fact, Psalm 19:1 says, "The heavens declare the glory of God."

Those who have never visited the Grand Canyon[8] still usually have a preconceived opinion of what it looks like. But those who have visited it describe an astounding "masterpiece" that cannot be comprehended unless actually experienced personally.

Before I saw the Grand Canyon I thought, "Yeah, yeah! It's a big hole in the ground." But, when I stepped off of the tour bus and began to take in its beauty and immensity, it literally took my breath away. I didn't realize that nature could have that effect on me. I remember thinking, "Ooooh! This is incredible!"

And all the Grand Canyon is, is a big hole! But there is just something about nature that says, "Look at God!" "Look what He can do!" "Look what He made!"

What an extraordinary experience it must be to travel in space. What an amazing encounter with God's creation! It makes sense why scientists at NASA become so excited when observing the stars, the galaxies, and all of the formations and interactions in the entirety of outer space -- that HUGE expanse of infinite proportions!

So, that which is observed and experienced in God's created world tells about Him. Therefore, *Nature* is certainly a way that God has revealed Himself to us. But God has also used other methods to reveal Himself.

---

[8] All images taken by Orion Lawlor and placed completely in the public domain. http://charm.cs.uiuc.edu/users/olawlor/photos/places/Arizona/2004/grand_canyon.

GOD HAS REVEALED HIMSELF THROUGH HIS SON

When God sent **His Son**,[9] Christ Jesus, to Earth, God told us more about Himself. He provided us with a tangible figure that could be observed interacting with all of man's natural activities. He furnished us with a glimpse of what perfection in manhood looks like and another evidence of what God is like. Since Christ is God, Christ revealed God to man.

GOD HAS REVEALED HIMSELF THROUGH MIRACLES

We also presuppose another method of revelation in **Miracles!** Christ raised Lazarus (John 11). He changed water into wine (John 2). He healed many sick and afflicted people. God used miracles to tell us about Himself -- His awesome power, His caring nature, etc.

---

[9] Pictures of Jesus and raising of Lazarus from free Bible clipart http://www.searchingthescriptures.net, accessed 1/28/11.

GOD HAS REVEALED HIMSELF THROUGH DIRECT CONVERSATION/SPEAKING

Sometimes God the Father has *talked* directly to man or through His angels to man. When God spoke to Moses through the burning bush,[10] he was using direct communication (Exod. 3, 4). Both through the words that He spoke and through His method, God was saying, "Moses, let me tell you who I am and what I want you to do!" God also spoke directly to Abraham (Gen. 17), to Saul/Paul (Acts 9) and others. He used direct conversation to tell man about Himself.

GOD HAS REVEALED HIMSELF THROUGH THE BIBLE –

HIS WORD

The last of God's revelations of Himself is through **His Word -- the Bible**.[11] As Christians, we accept that fact. If we want to get to know God better, we need to know what His Word says about Him. The Reverend John MacArthur said, "If I can't trust the Bible fully, then I can't trust what it says about God."[12] So we have to start with that belief because it is upon an inerrant word that the rest of our faith is learned and built. "All scripture is God-breathed and is useful for teaching, rebuking, correcting and training in righteousness..." (2 Tim. 3:16). What are the implications that that belief has?

---

[10] Picture of Moses and Burning Bush (Item: #25339617) purchased and downloaded from clipart.com, 2/1/11.

[11] Picture of Bible (Item: #21657587) purchased from clipart.com, 2/1/11.

[12] John MacArthur, "The Josiah Grauman Story"
http://billsbible.blogspot.com/2009/09/josiah-grauman-story-john-macarthur.html.
(Posted Wednesday, September 09, 2009), Accessed 28 Sept. 2009.

THE BIBLE DEALS WITH REAL PEOPLE WITH REAL FEELINGS AND ACTIONS!

It is remarkable how pertinent the Bible is to our everyday lives. It has something to say about life's most important issues -- relationships, marriage, depression, anxiety. It is all in there -- even though we often forget to look there for help with those issues. Or sometimes, we don't have the eyes to see the answers given. We may read a particular passage without thinking, "Wait a minute! What is it that Hezekiah was feeling there?"

When God went to Moses and said, "I want you to go and lead my people out," what did Moses do (Exod. 3, 4)? He argued with God! "Uhhh . . . You really don't want me. You see, I'm not a good public speaker. I don't do that real well. So . . . uh . . . You probably want somebody else."

So God went into a lengthy discourse and said, "No, Moses, I want you and I'm going to give you what you need. I made you. I made your mouth. I know what you are capable of."

And Moses continued, "Okay, I hear you God. But, there's another problem. Nobody's going to believe me! They're going to say, 'Who are you?' and 'Who sent you?' and 'How do we know that?' And . . . I'm not a real believable kind of guy."

What you hear is *self-contempt*! And yet GOD is talking to him! Just start taking apart that story. What an amazing story! God is talking to him. Moses is looking at a miracle -- the burning bush, and he's ARGUING with God based on his self-contempt!

"You don't want me! I tried that 40 years ago. It didn't work out so well! I've been in the desert now. It's pretty comfortable. And, I just wondered if it would be okay if I could just stay here."

Finally, God got kind of aggravated with him and said, "Well, fine! I'll send your brother, Aaron, with you and he'll help you."

And Moses kind of went, "Okay."

You can see all kinds of psychology in there! God's word is FULL of people, real people, who are struggling, and trying to figure things out, and making a mess of their lives, and then trying to find the right way to go!

And then, look at David. The story of his life provides ALL kinds of psychological data -- unfair treatment, success, failures, family problems, highs and lows, etc. But, you have to have eyes to see it and to look at Scripture and say, "Oh, I think there's something more there than simply a systematic theology or simply a story. There is a lot going on there." They were REAL people that felt just like we do!

THE BIBLE IS A GOOD AND HELPFUL BOOK

And notice what the rest of 2 Timothy 3:16 says: The Bible is profitable "for doctrine, for reproof, for correction, and for instruction" (KJV). It's a good book! AND the book tells us something about God's design. So we ought to learn the book to know God's design. That's what we're going to try to do.

5. God Made People in His Image and Likeness

Not only did God create us, but the Bible says that God created us in His image and in His likeness. We are going[13] to try to figure out what that means because we have a problem: God told us in six different passages, "I made you in My likeness/image" (Gen. 1:26, 27), yet He doesn't tell us what that means.

Nowhere in the Bible are we told what it means to be in the "image" and "likeness" of God, so numerous theologians have given varied ideas of what those words mean. Different views of "image" and "likeness" will be

---

[13] Painting by Michelangelo (Michelangelo di Lodovico Buonarroti Simoni) @ 1511 fresco, Sistine Chapel, Vatican City.

examined in Chapter 3 along with the effect that being created in God's "image" and "likeness" has on "Personality"; but for now, "image" and "likeness" will be assumed -- even though we may not fully understand what that means. We are made in God's "image" and "likeness."

Our view of the image and likeness of God influences our thinking and behavior.

One way that happens is that **we have a respect for human beings** -- ALL human beings, no matter how "bad" they are. We have an intrinsic respect for people. So even though we don't think highly of criminals, as sincere Christians we may decide to pray for them.

Taking the time to do something that may benefit the wicked, goes against man's natural inclination. The tendency is to just want to hate evil people! The desire is to see them be punished! And though the Bible does demonstrate that there is a time for punishment of and/or separation from unrepentant sinners, there is something about being in the image and likeness of God that gives us a respect for human beings. That respect says, "I want your salvation. I want you to have what I have."

6. We Represent God -- Though Sinfully/Imperfectly

Now we move to Presupposition number 6. Part of what it means to be in the image and likeness of God is that God says, "You are to represent Me. You are my ambassadors here on Earth. You are to represent Me and to represent Me well."

After God created man, a problem came in. Sin entered. It changed how man represented God. People no longer have the FULL capacity to represent God well.

Now some say, "Sin MARRED the image of God." Though that is commonly used terminology -- especially among theologians, it is not always clear what that means. We may know what it means to "mar" a statue. -- Someone or something breaks off the nose or the arm, etc. But, what does it mean to "mar" the image and likeness of God?

The problem could be summarized by saying: We don't represent God well. We don't have the full capacity to represent God well, the way we used to.

Because of sin, we are now corrupted. We are "depraved." But what does that mean?

Depravity is a concept that is sometimes misunderstood. Depravity, or being fully depraved, doesn't mean you're as sinful as you can be.

Even Hitler had days when he chose to do "nice" things. He had a female companion. He must have treated her well enough that she decided to "stick around." He picked up children and hugged them. He put food on people's tables! He had seemingly good moments! The horrific, evil things that he did are well known, but he wasn't as BAD as he could have been!

Depravity simply means, "We're as BAD OFF as we can be." In the sight of God, we're in deep trouble -- and all it takes is ONE sin! Every human being misses the mark of perfection. So it does not mean we are as BAD as we can be; but it does mean we are as BAD OFF as we can be. Some major consequences of sin keep us from a relationship with God and keep us from following His design. Yet we still have characteristics that represent God, though those characteristics can "bend" in sinful directions. As Christians, we have the opportunity to use those characteristics for good as we strive to represent God well.

7. People are Held Accountable to God.
We are Personally Responsible for Our Sins.

Sometimes we think we are pretty good and we can become proud of our accomplishments. That is not to say that we shouldn't feel good about being productive and useful; but what does our righteousness without Christ look like to God?

Isaiah 64:6 paints an abhorrent mental picture for us. It says, "Our righteousness is as . . . filthy rags." The passage is actually comparing our righteousness to menstrual rags.

The context of the passage refers specifically to the Israelites in Isaiah's time who were not following God. It is interesting to note that Isaiah includes himself in this passage, showing that this truth could be applied to the entire human race.

All of us are declared "unclean" and our righteous acts (even the best of them) have "become like a garment stained with menstrual discharge."[14] This passage is quite strong. It compares righteousness to a soiled, feminine hygiene product that is repulsive to God. This is the best we can do without God.

Even as Christians, our righteousness looks like that. Now, praise God that because of salvation, we will not receive the consequences for it, but even as Christians our sin can be pretty ugly.

PEOPLE WHO SEEM TO BE "NICE"
ARE NOT ALWAYS GOOD CHRISTIANS

Now, there are people -- Christians, even so-called Christians, and non-Christians -- who are very "NICE-LOOKING" people. Some of them may also lead us to believe that they are really "good" -- not possessing that filthy core -- and to us they may look "good." But remember Christ's words concerning the Pharisees in Matthew 23 and other passages? What about motive? What about thinking? What about things that are under the surface -- they look good on the outside, but maybe underneath is there something else going on? Proverbs 20:5 addresses the fact that knowing "the purposes of a man's heart" can be difficult because they are "deep waters." Yet the Bible says that "a man of understanding draws them out."

When living our lives as Christians in this world, we need to be aware that though we all still have a sin nature and are dependent on God's grace for entrance to heaven, there are some who lead us to believe that they don't possess any sinfulness or very little of it. They may even be very convincing as they cite their attainment of high Christian values without acknowledging fault. Those are the ones that Christ warns us about. When you understand the "psychology" of what is going on (of which the entire Bible cites specific incidences over and over again), then you can be "armed" with the weapons (Eph. 6:10-18) to recognize and attack the evil that may be intent on "sucking" you in. When you are in relationship with those who never acknowledge specific sins -- who rationalize away the wrong that they do and seem to be intent on "selling" themselves as godly

---

[14] C.F. Keil & F. Delitzsche, *Commentary on the Old Testament*, *VII* (Grand Rapids: Wm. B. Eerdmans Publishing Co., 1975) p. 470.

– beware! When people promote themselves, reluctant to humbly acknowledge their failures to others, the Bible says of that type in Mark 8:15, "'Be careful . . . Watch out for the yeast of the Pharisees . . .'" (All of us have a desire to overlook our own faults, so having that tendency is not what is being referred to here. The godly person will "catch" himself many times and humble himself by acknowledging his sin. The ungodly person refuses to look at his wrongdoing when directly confronted or even over time, and tends to find convincing ways to rationalize his sin away.)

So what we need to realize and assume as Christians is that we DO still have a sin nature (Romans 7) and we are responsible for that sin. We need to confess that sin and humbly offer our wretched selves to God. We need to take responsibility for what is ours. It is there in everyone. Understanding that concept helps prevent our being "fooled" by those who can present a convincing "front."

Ezekiel 18 is a passage that points out responsibility. In this passage, it is saying, "No, it's not what your father or your grandfather did. It is you." You are going to be held accountable only for you. Though it is true that other generations can cause you problems and, because of their sin, they can do things that damage you that can go on or have gone on for several generations. But YOU can break the cycle.

So part of responsibility is a good thing -- not just that we are responsible for our own sins, but also that we can do something about them. We can make things better. We can break the cycle. We don't have to do to the next generation what our parents did to us.

So what are the implications for the Christian? And how do Christians respond to their own victimization or the "victim" mentality of someone else?

THE "VICTIM" MENTALITY

If we were victimized as children, does that take away our responsibility as Christians? Can we blame any of our present condition on that victimization?

First of all, we all have been victimized -- some much worse than others. Some have been victimized in dreadful ways and that should not be overlooked or minimized. But, the fact of the matter is that all of us have gone through some sort of victimization. If we didn't get it at home, we got it at school. All of us can tell stories of ways we were hurt by other kids . . . ways we were hurt by other adults . . . by people who were supposed to be leading, who were supposed to be caring for us, looking after us . . . even by people in the church – sometimes "spiritual" people. We can all tell stories of how we have been victimized.

We are not responsible for that. We are not responsible for what our parents did to us . . . what a teacher did to us . . . what the Boy Scout leader did to us. We are not responsible for people who victimized us. We are not responsible for our victimization and how we were treated by others.

But we ARE responsible for **how we deal with** our victimization. How will we think about that? What choices will we make around that? How will we behave given that? We may not be able to control certain emotions that come up, but what do we choose to do with those emotions? Now, we are talking about responsibility!

Some people talk like they are total victims, given their situation. "There's nothing I can do." "Sorry, I hit you. Hey, I'm a victim." " Sorry I yelled at you. I'm a victim. There's nothing I can do about it."

We should rather be saying, "My parents did this to me and they were wrong. Now, what do I want to do about that? How do I want to interact with others in a way that is different from my parents? How can I give to others the love and affirmation that I didn't get? Yeah, I'll hold my parents responsible for what they did, but what will I do in response to that?" That is the KEY!

Sinfulness is deep in the core of all of us, and one of the ways it emerges is in deferring responsibility and "playing the victim." We like "playing the victim" and avoiding responsibility because taking responsibility exposes us to the possibility of consequences that may be uncomfortable or even painful. So where we need to be focused, as Christians, is going to a place that is hard for us to go -- taking time to look at our sin, taking responsibility, and saying, "Will you please forgive me?"

That can be a tough thing to do. But taking responsibility and acknowledging personal sin is something that we must do and is the basis for the Christian life (1 John 1:9).

The lack of responsibility is also something that drives away the non-Christian community faster than anything else. No one likes a hypocrite, and non-Christians become especially disillusioned and angered by people who claim to be Christians and yet do not take responsibility when they are wrong or defend themselves in an attempt to appear "faultless." As Christians, it is paramount for our growth and for our impact in our community that we take responsibility for our sin and seek forgiveness.

8. There is Salvation from Sin

But God provided a solution to the devastating sin problem: He provided salvation from sin. Because of Christ dying on the cross, all we have to do is ask, and the burden of our sin is gone (John 3:16, etc.)

When Christ died for us, He justified us (declared to be righteous) and sanctified us (set apart from sin) (1 Cor. 6:11). Those two words explain what Christ did and what He continues to do for us. Those effects of Christ's death are extremely important aspects of our salvation and of the Christian life.

9. New Life in Christ[15]

And after salvation, there is new life in Christ. Take a look at the photo of Mt. St. Helens in Washington State. Though the volcano caused severe devastation to the countryside after its eruption in 1980, it didn't take long for new life to appear. New life came out of destruction! Out of all of the ash and

[15] MSH84_st_helens_from_harrys_ridge_fireweed_august_1984.jpg.
http://vulcan.wr.usgs.gov/Volcanoes/MSH/Images/recovery.html. The maps, graphics, images, and text found on our website, unless stated otherwise, are within the Public Domain. Credit back to the USGS/Cascades Volcano Observatory is appreciated. "Fireweed is one species of plant life which has returned to Mount St. Helens' devastated area. Vegetation began reappearing as early as the summer of 1980 as many small trees and plants were protected by the snowpack on May 18. Seeds, carried by the wind or by animals, also entered the area and grew. By 1985, the ridges surrounding the volcano were covered with new growth." USGS Photograph taken in August 1984, by Lyn Topinka.

devastation, look what happened. Though the pinks and greens aren't shown here, do you see what is growing up out of all of that mess? It is hard to fathom the transformation to a beautiful landscape and the return of animal life after such ruin.

The same is true in our lives. As we deal with sin and all of its consequences, a beauty can emerge.

As Joseph said, "What you meant for evil, God meant for good" (Gen. 50:20). And look what happened! Look at what God did and continues to do!

You can always start anew. You can always build on the mistakes or hurts of the past and allow God to make something new and better. You can "help" because you know what "hurt" looks like.

You have new life -- not only to live as a Christian, but since you have been unencumbered by the load of the Law and sin, you can say, "Look at what God did!" There is hope! There is new life!

Because of your understanding of what Christ did for you, you can say, "I thank God for bringing me through those hard times and those sinful times. Without my realization of that sin and without those hurts, I wouldn't have the ability to understand others in the way that I do now. I couldn't touch those people's lives without that. And I wouldn't have the joy of living in Christ that I have now, had I not had a need and seen how Christ could fulfill it."

10. Life Has One Fundamental Purpose: To Please God

Lastly, life has one fundamental purpose, and that is to please God. "Whatever you eat, or drink, or whatever you do, do all to the glory of God" (1 Corinthians 10:31).

As Christians, we always know why we are here. We always know our purpose -- to please God. We were "built" to please Him.

Whether we sell insurance, teach school, counsel, work in a factory, farm land, raise children, etc., it doesn't matter; whatever we do as Christians, our purpose is to please God. Some of the ways we can do that are by working hard, praying, and loving people well. If we realize that our one purpose is to please God, we always have a reason for living and a goal to strive for. That purpose can be accomplished through each of our unique personalities in various ways. And it is true in every situation that we find ourselves. We can always make a choice to please God.

Final Thoughts
WHAT WE BRING TO THE TABLE

Now that the foundation of presuppositions has been laid, here are a few final thoughts to ponder.

If you are a Christian, you probably held to most of the previously discussed presuppositions even before you ever began reading this material. It could be that you would alter the wording a bit. You may add a few more presuppositions to the ones mentioned. But probably, you would be willing to say with conviction that, "I believe there is a God," "I believe that He has given us the Bible as His revelation," and "I believe that the Bible ought to be our guideline for life."

It is important for us as Christians to understand what we bring to the table. That is what we believe. And that will affect how we think and how we live our lives.

THE END OF EVERY ARGUMENT

We base our beliefs on faith. Our faith makes sense to us because God has revealed it to us. Yet others may not accept what seems to be so clearly evident to us. Though it may seem that we can "convince" others, it may be helpful to realize that our presuppositions are the end of every argument or discussion that we encounter.

Presuppositions are not the BEGINNING of every argument even though they are "pre" suppositions. Presuppositions are the END of every argument. Why might that be true?

If someone who believed in evolution[16] came to you right now and said, "Here is all of the data we have as to why we believe evolution to be true" . . . if he presented a compelling case for evolution and determined that there was NO supernatural force behind it at all, would you believe it?

---

[16] Reference is to Darwinian Evolution – the theory that we all came from one common ancestor and as changes occurred over time we have what we have today. Most Christians would say that God created specific kinds (multiple ancestors) – one being human. An evolution that involves small-scale changes and not a common ancestor could be a part of a Creationist view, but typically when people think of Evolution, they think of the Darwinian Evolution.

If you espouse to the previous ten presuppositions, you would say, "No!"

Why not? Maybe he has good arguments and good charts, graphs, and pictures. Why wouldn't you believe it?

You would probably respond with something like this, "I know what you're telling me. I hear it. You've got some compelling arguments. But, I don't believe it."

Have you ever had an argument with someone like that . . . when you knew you were right!? Maybe you had done some research. Maybe you saw something on TV. Maybe you witnessed the event in person, and yet your observation was discounted.

Some people still believe that the earth is flat. In fact, there is a "Flat Earth Society." People in that society believe that the earth is not a sphere. It is not circular. It is flat.[17]

If you spoke with someone in that group, he may say to you, "Hey! Just go out there and look. There's no curvature!" He may walk and walk in his effort to prove it to you and continue to declare, "It's flat!"

In the early 1960s, when the Mercury spaceships were sent into space; astronauts took pictures which showed that the earth was ROUND! However, some STILL denied that fact!

One such naysayer asked, "What kind of camera did they use?

The answer, "Well, just a regular camera."

He continued, "What kind of lens did it have on it?"

"Well, you know, a round lens."

"Okay! There you have it!" he said.

That was his argument for why the earth looked round in the pictures. He thought the 'round' lens produced the 'illusion' that the earth was round! And so, he was still convinced and steadfastly maintained his belief that the earth was flat.[18]

You may have heard the story of the man who thought he was dead. So someone poked his skin with a needle until he bled and then said, "See,

---

[17] Documentation of the existence of the "Flat Earth Society" found at http://www.alaska.net/~clund/e_djublonskopf/Flatearthsociety.htm. Documentation found on 1/4/09.

[18] The "naysayer" was the great grandfather of the primary author.

you're bleeding!" But, the man responded, "Oh, I guess dead people DO bleed."

Now, whether that story is true or not, it still illustrates the point very well. Presuppositions are the end of every argument. When all is said and done, when it comes right down to it, the most important question is, "What do you believe?"

The question is not who has the most compelling data. Though at times we run across compelling data and change our beliefs, many times our beliefs are just our beliefs. There are certain things that we simply believe.

It is important for us to be aware of this -- that sometimes we're going to say, "Here's what I think," and the person listening will say, "I don't believe that. I think my way is right."

If that is what he or she believes, that is just what he/she is going to believe.

Be aware of what you "bring to the table" and that some of the people that you deal with may not bring the same presuppositions. And, if you want to give information, that's fine, but they may say, "I don't buy that! I'm not interested."

Does that mean we can't befriend those with whom we disagree or have a positive impact on them? No. We are just going to have two different sets of presuppositions, and we are going to have to find some common ground to try to talk together. Hopefully one day they will say, "I'd like to hear more about your presuppositions." Then we have a chance to tell them.

That can be our prayer and our hope for those who are unsaved. But it is important to understand what our presuppositions are and what theirs are and realize that they are not always the same.

Presuppositions are powerful! They will determine our eternal destination! Think about that. What you believe will determine where you spend eternal life -- heaven or hell. That is how powerful they are. What you believe will determine how you behave and how you feel. Presuppositions are that powerful.

So here is where we are moving. In the next section entitled, "Integration," we will be looking to answer the question: "Can we take anything from secular psychology?" Can we take anything from secular theorists -- who don't believe in our presuppositions, who don't believe in the Bible, and who don't believe in God? We need to understand that there are intelligent people whom God has gifted in many ways, who may draw faulty conclusions from observed data because of their presuppositions. But can we take information from those astute, secular theorists who have made observations, yet who have different presuppositions than we do? The next chapter, entitled "Integration," will attempt to address those questions as they pertain to Christians and our Christian belief system.

CHAPTER 2

INTEGRATION

We now focus on the questions that concluded the previous chapter: Can we take anything from secular psychology? Can we take anything from secular theorists who don't believe in our presuppositions, who don't believe in the Bible, and who don't believe in God?

There are a number of people in the Christian community who would say that integration is not appropriate for the Christian when it comes to the subject of psychology. Much of their determination regarding integration is based on good reasoning. Teachings of some in the field of psychology do not match up with biblical principles and Christian beliefs.

How do you bring together the view that the Bible is the inerrant, inspired word of God and the belief of one who says, "The book has some relevance, but is not all that important," or "It's just a book and has no importance," or "It's a group of myths -- put together over the years. People invented it and invented the religion that came out of it"? How does one put those viewpoints together and say, "We're going to integrate that"? The two concepts are mutually exclusive.

"There is a God. God created. The world is His design. His design works."

"No, there is no God. We're here by evolutionary forces. It's just time and chance. Given enough time, given enough evolutionary forces -- matter floating around, gases floating around and coming together -- it happened."

How does one integrate those positions? If the intention is to put those two ideas together, obviously, it is impossible. The ideas are mutually exclusive.

Integration of Theology and Psychology

Integration: not a good term

Christian	Secular
Inerrant, inspired Word of God	Book with some or no relevance
Creation: God's design	Evolution: time chance
Life Goal: glorifying God (I Cor. 10:31)	Life Goal: coping and adapting

For the Christian, 1 Corinthians 10:31 defines our purpose for living. Life is all about glorifying God, "Whether you eat or drink or whatever you do, do it all for the glory of God." This is a foundational belief.

What is life all about in the secular world? Without God, it is all about *survival* -- "coping and adapting." Survival is the goal and in order to survive, you have to cope and adapt to your environment. That is the essence of the evolutionary-based belief of our secular world.

So, *integration*, if it means bringing together two opposing sets of beliefs and trying to make them become one perspective, does not appear to be a suitable approach for the Christian. It isn't something that can happen. It makes sense then why some Christians say it shouldn't be done. But what some then conclude is: "Let's throw out psychology."

This conclusion often seems to stem from an underlying belief that psychology consists of the *theories* that have been produced by psychologists, rather than the true definition of psychology. Psychology is merely the study of mind and behavior. Psychology involves the study of all of those things connected with the mind. In addition to the biology of the brain, psychology involves thought processes, emotions, learning, memory, worry, stress, and the behavior that results from the workings of the mind. If one starts with that as a definition of psychology, it will be easier to understand the basis for the concepts developed in this book. The intention of this book is to build a platform for understanding the thinking and behavior of man and to reveal what the Bible has to say about those faculties.

Can You Take Psychology Out of the Bible?

If we look at psychology as thinking and behavior, is it possible to take psychology out of the Bible? Wouldn't that be like taking out all of the nouns in the Bible or taking out all of the history in the Bible or taking out all of the lessons in the Bible? It can't be done. The nouns and the history and the lessons are all important parts of the Bible message. Without them, the Bible doesn't exist. They are all needed to communicate the message that God has intended for us to get. In fact, one may think that he has eliminated psychology from the Bible; but if he still believes what is written, he has only discarded the *label*, "psychology," not the existence of psychology.

You can't take the psychology out of the Bible. You can't take out all of the thinking and behaviors, just like you can't take all of the nouns out of the Bible and still communicate the message. You can't tell the story without nouns. You can change the label "nouns" to something else, but they are still nouns. They still name persons, places, or things. The same is true with the "psychology" in the Bible. Psychology (mind and behavior) is inherent in the Bible message.

Are All Secularists' Teachings Wrong?

But that is only one of the issues that needs to be dealt with in regard to psychology and the Christian. Even though we may be aware that a psychology of the Bible exists, what do we do about all of the "psychology" apart from the Bible? What do we do about all of those theories and secular psychologists that address different psychological topics?

Take a minute and return to the idea held by some that psychology is the *theories* that psychologists have proposed and assume that those theories were proposed by secular theorists. Or suppose that psychology is the research that secular psychologists have conducted. Would that now mean that we should throw out all of psychology because the information came from a secular psychologist?

And even though we know that psychology *isn't* the theories or research, we still must address the question of what to do with the information that is dispersed from secular psychologists. Can Christians learn anything from secular psychologists? Is everything learned and reported or theorized by secular psychologists, wrong?

"Let's throw out anything that is secular, because somehow it's bad. It's tainted. It's not what God wants." Is that what Christians need to conclude? -- Probably not.

But, it does bring up some important questions. First of all, if the presuppositions of Christians and non-Christians are mutually exclusive, does secular psychology have anything *good* to offer?

Or consider this: Can secular psychologists and theorists, stumble upon biblical truth? Could they observe the world and find truth? That is worth pondering.

If they can (and the Bible seems to indicate that they can -- Prov. 29:13, 1 Cor. 15:33), is it legitimate for us to borrow from them? Can we use their material? Is it okay to acknowledge the truths that they have found?

Cognitive Therapy emphasizes that thinking is vitally important. Could the cognitive therapist have stumbled on truth when choosing to look into man's thinking? Could he have stumbled on truth while seeking to know what the source of man's emotions and behavior is? Proverbs 23:7 says, "For as he thinketh in his heart/*soul* (translated in NASB "within himself"), so is he" (KJV). Did the cognitive therapists happen to learn something that the Bible teaches? If you are familiar with Freud's "Defense Mechanisms," you realize that Freud made a keen observation that makes sense. Looking at Freud's explanation of defense mechanisms and then going to Scripture, one may be surprised to realize that some can be found there. Though unregenerate and some of his theories reflect that unregenerate mindset, Freud was also able to notice things that were true. Yet it was the same person, Freud, who came up with the Oedipal Complex and other theories that contradict Christian teaching.

Did Freud create defense mechanisms? No. Defense mechanisms have been around since sin entered the human race. But Freud drew attention to them and noticed what techniques people use to try to defer blame or unpleasant feelings. He put a label on them so that we could study them and think through what they are accomplishing for us in life. Could those "defense mechanisms" have been found if one had not read Freud? -- Maybe. -- But maybe not. -- Maybe not to the same degree to which Freud described them.

So studying psychology and then checking out that information with Scripture can cause us to think in ways that we haven't thought before and find things that we may not have found otherwise. Can we reclaim those things and say, "Freud found some biblical truths"?

Freud labeled one of his defense mechanisms, "projection." It is not called that in the Bible, but could it still be a real mechanism employed by people to hide what is going on inside? And could one use Freud's material on "Projection" to understand human nature a little bit better?

An attentive Christian may find that there are many pieces of information that secularists have "stumbled upon" through God's enlightenment that are very true and quite useful. And Scripture even supports the fact that unbelievers can come up with truth -- as demonstrated in the verses previously mentioned – Proverbs 29:13 and I Corinthians 15:33 (where Paul quotes the philosopher/poet, Menander).

Dangerous?

However, can taking information from secularists be dangerous? Can we be led astray by unbelieving theorists?

Well, can Christians be led astray by the world? Of course! The Bible makes it clear that we can be misled. (That is part of the psychology of how our minds work and how things can influence us for evil.) That is why the Bible gives us parameters for dealing with our world. God wants us to maintain our relationships with Christians (by not "forsaking the assembling of ourselves together," Heb. 10:25). God wants us to "think about such things" that are true, noble, right, pure, lovely, and admirable (Phil. 4: 8). God wants us to meditate on His laws "day and night" (Ps. 1). God's word warns us about forming unhealthy relationships with those who practice bad habits and sin blatantly -- "Bad company corrupts good morals" (I Cor. 15:33), and it communicates to us that a steady diet of sinful exposure can influence us in negative ways in Proverbs and other passages. The Bible warns over and over of lurking temptation, teachings, and evil people who are waiting to "devour us" with their wickedness.

Immersing ourselves in any secular teachings alone without a firm biblical base can be dangerous. If we haven't equipped ourselves with the "armor of God" (Ephesians 6), it becomes more difficult to ward off the evil teachings and to make wise decisions. That is why we need a firm biblical base in order to function in our world at all. That is why we need to understand the advice that Paul gives in order to "stand firm" (Phil. 4:1). No matter what we do, no matter what profession we pursue, no matter what activities we get involved in, we need to know what God teaches and how to deal with ourselves and our world (2 Tim. 2:15).

So is it dangerous to go to a baseball game? Could I learn bad habits from a player or someone in the stands? Yes, possibly. Is it dangerous to watch TV? It could be. Is it dangerous to listen to music? -- Maybe. Is it dangerous to read observations recorded by a secularist? -- Perhaps.

But could we also learn something from a secularist that would be helpful to our lives? Yes, it is possible! Is it not within the realm of God's ability to use secularists to actually help us know God better and serve God better? Yes!

Most Christians agree that contributions by secularists in the medical world have merit and are worth studying -- even though the medical world can also promote things that Christians often oppose such as abortion, embryonic stem cell research, and euthanasia. But some of the very same Christians that accept information from the medical world are opposed to studying psychology.

So what makes the difference in our thinking? Whether we are studying medicine or psychology, how do we know what information and approaches we should accept and which ones we should oppose? In order to make the best judgments to discern what is appropriate and in order to make the best use of the secularists' teachings, we need to have a good biblical understanding.

Better Word Than Integration?

If we accept the idea that there *are* things that secularists can contribute to the Christian life, how would we define our use of that material? Does the word "integration" fit? Integration is the most commonly used word, yet it implies different things to different people. The discussions in this chapter will focus on the varying views that are implicated by the word "integration."

But, before looking at those views, it might be important here to consider the appropriateness of the term "integration" when it comes to discussing psychology and the Bible. Is "integration" the best word to describe what the Christian should do with information discovered by secularists? Or is there a better way to communicate what we mean when we speak of including the truths of secular teachings? Is there a better word than "integration"?

Integration is a word that conjures up connotations of our previous discussion of combining truth and non-truth which, it was determined, cannot be done. So, maybe it is not the best word to use. But, if "integration" is not a good term, what wording could be used to describe the usefulness of some secular teachings without accepting those pieces of information that are untrue and sometimes against what God's word teaches?

It could be that no *one* word can accurately describe the procedure that is involved when the Christian attempts to incorporate the truths found in the secular world (as they relate to psychology) into his own thinking. There may not be one word that can summarize what he is trying to do.

Proposed in this book is a group of words to describe the best method for Christians to use when taking truths discovered by secularists and using them. The group of words proposed in this book is: "Scriptural Foundation, Secular Nuggets." That wordage will be explained in the last of the five views examined next.

FIVE VIEWS OF INTEGRATION

What are the different views of "integration" -- if that term is going to be used? When people think of integration, what are the views that are most commonly assumed? Views of integration seem to fall into one of these five categories: 1) Facts, Not Faith; 2) The Word, Not Worldly Wisdom; 3) Accept Both, Integrate Neither; 4) The Two-Book View; and 5) Scriptural Foundation, Secular Nuggets.

1. Facts, Not Faith

In the first view, one is looking for scientific facts. That inquiry alone for "facts" tends to eliminate this as a true view of integration. The view basically says: "Theology isn't scientific. Throw it out." Only scientific psychology can be trusted, not theology, because theology is based on faith, a "non-trustable entity."

The view assumes that psychology is built upon empiricism. (The main pillar of science is empiricism: We bring things through our senses and make sense of those things.) Theology (they say) is built upon "non-science" (some would say "nonsense"). They say, "It's built upon 'faith'; therefore, theology ought to be rejected." Whatever is "nonscientific" is rejected, because "We're looking for *facts*!"

So the next question is: "Are there facts?" Do true "facts" exist? Can

---

[19] Clip Art from clker.com -- Public domain. "Microscope" By: Mohamed Ibrahim, Jan. 2011.

I say, "I know this to be 100% true and there is NOTHING that could disprove it?!" (That is how "fact" is being defined here.) Can anyone know things to be 100% true?

OUR SENSES CAN DECEIVE US

Consider the information that comes through our senses. Is that information 100% fool-proof? Are any or all of those things that come through our senses, facts? That is the concept that the "Scientific Method" is based upon -- bringing things through our senses and making sense of those things. But can we trust our senses?

Take a look at the following diagram.

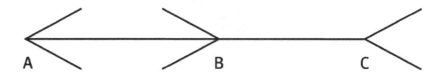

Which line appears to be longer? A to B or B to C?

The answer that your senses will usually tell you is: B to C is longer. But if you measure the lines; you would find that your senses were wrong! Your senses deceived you!

This is also true with airline pilots. They are trained to use instruments[20] to fly because sometimes their sense of position and motion fails to be accurate. They can have the illusion of being straight and level when almost nearly inverted or tumbling end over end when actually straight and level.[21] It is called "spatial disorientation"[22] and is caused by visual references being unclear or by the disturbance of fluid in the inner ear due to the Coriolus Effect.[23]

Another example is when you are stopped at a traffic light and the car beside you inches forward. It can cause you to feel like you are going backwards.

Sometimes our senses deceive us. What looks like truth is not always truth. In looking at the two lines, one looks longer. When considering what direction we are going or how level we are in an airplane, we can feel convinced that we are in one position when we are actually in another. Our senses can "play tricks" on us.

---

[20] http://www.wingweb.co.uk/Images/561/Northrop_Tacit_Blue_cockpit. This image is in the Public Domain, and may be re-used. Attribution is requested - please use "USAF" for attribution.

[21] Free Stock Photo of Cockpit of Air Fighter – Vehicles   http://www.public-domain-photos.com/vehicles/cockpit-of-air-fighter-4.htm

[22] <http://www.aopa.org/asf/publications/sa17.pdf> (Accessed January 5, 2009).

[23]Richard Seaman, "RNZAF A4 Skyhawk Team Tricks" <http://www.richard-seaman.com/Aircraft/AirShows/RNZAF/Skyhawks/TeamTricks/index.html> (5 January 2009).

The 1999 movie, *The Matrix*, based its entire plot on such deception.[24] The premise of the movie is that what looks like reality is really a software program and the true reality is outside the Matrix. Of course, we don't believe we are part of the Matrix; but can we prove that absolutely? No, just like we can't prove Heaven to an unbeliever. Sometimes even empiricism fails us. Because it cannot be proven through what they can currently see or touch, the idea of Heaven and Hell seem as ludicrous to the unbeliever as being in the Matrix seems to us. [25]

Those who believe that truth can be proven through empiricism need to be careful. Sometimes our senses deceive us and we assume truth that is not necessarily truth. And yet other times we are aware of things that other people aren't aware of, that might be true.

In studies involving witnesses to a crime, research has shown that eyewitnesses can even disagree on what actually happened, and they can be convinced that their perspective is the correct one.[26] Documentaries on the John F. Kennedy assassination that evaluate the angles of the bullet holes show that the shots could have only come from the Texas Depository Building. But some witnesses were convinced that shots were fired from a "grassy knoll."[27] What is the truth and could it be that people's senses were deceived? How do we know?

---

[24] Andy Wachowski & Larry Wachowski, *The Matrix*, Directed by Andy Wachowski, Larry Wachowski Producers: Andy Wachowski, Andrew Mason, Barrie M. Osborne, Bruce Berman (Studio: Warner Home Video, 1999).

[25] Author's note: It may be misconstrued by this discussion that I do not believe in absolute truth. I do believe in absolute truth, but notice that I have said, "I believe in absolute truth." I just can't absolutely prove it here on Earth.

[26] B. L. Cutler and S. D. Penrod, "Juror Decision Making in Eyewitness Identification Cases," *Law and Human Behavior* 12 (1988): 41-55. S. L. Sporer, R. S. Malpass, and G. Koehnken editors, *Psychological Issues in Eyewitness Identification*, (Mahwah, New Jersey: Erlbaum, 1996). G. L. Wells and E. A. Olson, "Eyewitness Testimony," *Annual Review of Psychology* 54 (2003) 277-295.

[27] www.msnbc.msn.com/id/27705829 "Tech puts JFK conspiracy theories to rest" *By Eric Bland* Discovery Channel -- updated 6:24 p.m. ET, Thurs., Nov. 13, 2008. (Accessed 1/5/09).

<www.spartacus.schoolnet.co.uk/JFKgrassyN.htm> -- Google's cache -- a snapshot of the page as it appeared on Dec 24, 2008 03:24:21 GMT. The current page could have changed in the meantime. (Accessed 1/5/09).

OUR RATIONALITY SOMETIMES DECEIVES US

If that's not compelling, we have other problems. Our rationality sometimes deceives us. Sometimes we have pretty good data, but we draw the wrong conclusions from that data.

In one of the Monty Python movies that emerged in the 1970s, there is a discussion about whether a particular woman is a witch.[28] The characters go through various aspects of evaluating the reality of that claim, such as the fact that you burn witches and wood also burns, so witches must be made of wood. Wood floats and so does a duck; so if she weighs the same as a duck, she must be a witch.

Now, is that scientific? Did you catch that logic? Why did we know she was a witch?

-- Because she weighed the same as a duck. Now we laugh at that, but how many times do we get good data and draw those kinds of conclusions in the scientific world?

A search on the Internet will produce a number of articles telling of fish fossils or sea life fossils found in places where water creatures and plants were not likely to be found -- such as at the top of a mountain. Even Charles Darwin found fish fossils on tops of mountains. How do you think they got there? What would be your theory?

As Christians, some of us immediately think that that is evidence of the Great Flood. But that is not the conclusion that was drawn by Charles Darwin when he observed that phenomenon[29] or by numerous others.

Though investigators can go into great lengths to present very elaborate data of the type of fossils and the type of fish and how it would have been highly unlikely for them to have inhabited that area at any time, and though the researchers can demonstrate detailed ways to measure the time and age of the fossils, the primary conclusion of some of the articles could be summarized like this: A meteor hit the ocean. It splashed the water up to the mountain. As a result of the "splashing," fish were thrust up to that remote, dry area at the top of the mountain. The fish flopped

---

[28] Graham Chapman, John Cleese, Eric Idle, Terry Gilliam, Terry Jones, and Michael Palin, *Monty Python and the Holy Grail*, Directed by Terry Gilliam and Terry Jones, Producer: Mark Forstater, Executive Producer: John Goldstone, (1975).

[29] *Charles Darwin*, "John Edmondstone," <http://www.taxidermy4cash.com/darwin.html> (accessed 5 January 2009).

around, and they died.[30]

Could that have happened? Or could it have been the Great Flood? Could it be that the mountain rose up from the ocean and brought the fish with them? What could have happened? How do we know? We weren't there. The conclusions drawn from that data can vary greatly -- especially from that of the Christian.

So that is the problem that can happen, even with collecting good data. The conclusion that seems rational to us based on our data may not be accurate. Our rationality can deceive us.

WHO IS GOING TO INTERPRET THE DATA?

But, if our rationality can deceive us, then how do we know if the interpretation of the data is accurate? Do we have someone that we know can evaluate the data correctly? Who is going to interpret the data for us? Are you going to interpret the data? Are you "trustable"? What about the leading scientists? Can we trust them? Might they have their biases and prejudices and backgrounds that influence and "slant" their interpretations?

So who is going to do it? Ultimately it comes down to "Me." Why? "Well, I trust me."

---

[30] Articles on the Internet regarding fish fossils on mountains and meteors causing fish fossils are numerous. Two such articles of fish fossils on mountains are: www.natureandscience.org/research/wyoming.asp and www.yellowstonetreasures.com/fish_fossils.htm. Other sites promoting the idea of meteors causing fish extinction are: www.nsf.gov/news/news_summ.jsp?cntn_id=100836&org=NSF&from=news and school.discoveryeducation.com/lessonplans/programs/livingfossils/ where a study unit is designed for students to discuss the various theories including the idea of a meteor causing the extinction of creatures such as fish and causing fish fossils. http://www.cps.org.yu/Innerpeace/Creation/noah.html. Paragraph 6, documents "marine" fossils on mountains.

Quote from Chapter 5, "The Hovind Theory," *cs.joensuu.fi/~vtenhu/hovind/CHP-5.htm* "Maybe it all happened because of the meteor hitting the earth. If hot water came shooting out of the earth's crust, it would cause some problems on earth. If you dumped a million gallons into a lake what would happen to the fish? It would kill them in an instance, wouldn't it? The reason would be due to a condition known as thermal shock. Fish have a certain temperature change that they can withstand per minute. If the temperature changes too quickly, it will kill them. Thermal shock would take place if hot water from beneath the ocean came shooting up into the ocean and it would kill things in the immediate vicinity."

That is where we are in the post-modern world. "I trust me; therefore my belief is right. And you have to respect that."

Now, treating others with respect is a godly way of behaving. And respecting others' beliefs can be considerate. But, just because you think you're right and they think they're right, does it follow that both of you are right? -- Obviously not.

If one answer is right and it excludes the other, then the other cannot also be right. If two people have opposing opinions, then it could be that one of them is right and one is wrong, or both could be wrong. But the idea that opposing opinions (opinions that are diametrically opposed to each other) could both be right, obviously, is impossible. If one says, "There is no God," and the other says, "There is a God," they both may think they are right; but in reality, they can't both be right. At least one of the answers always has to be wrong. You can't get away from it.

But my senses can deceive me. My rationality can deceive me. So the scientific method cannot assure me with certainty that what the scientists promote is right. They cannot prove their "facts" with absolute certainty and they cannot prove their interpretations either.

YOU CAN'T GET ALL OF THE DATA

Then there is another problem: You can't get all of the data. Even if we have the best methods in the world for gathering data, how do we know for sure that we have all of the data?

At one time, we thought that the table that we ate off of was totally solid. Our senses told us that and we trusted them. Now, with research and electron microscopes, we know that the table is made up of atoms, and atoms are mostly space. It is the speed of the electrons around the nucleus that makes the table appear solid. With more data, we realized that our perception was wrong.

At one time, people thought that everything revolved around the Earth; but with research, we found that the planets revolve around the sun. Again, our senses deceived us, and new data discredited the old theory.

We can never be sure that we have all of the data! And even though we have added much more data and know a lot more about the subject, there is always the possibility of new data. We can't get all of the data. We can't get all of the NEW data because tomorrow there is going to be more new data.

Some have said that to put our faith in research is like a spider building his house on the hands of a clock. As time passes, his house is continually destroyed.

As time passes, we always have new data, new theories, and those new theories sometimes discredit the old theories. So am I going to put my faith in theories that 20 years from now we may consider obsolete?

HOW DO YOU PROVE THE "PROVER"?

And lastly, how do you prove the "prover"? Assume that we have a method that proves a particular piece of information to be true. Now we have to prove that the method for proving that is true. Well, how do we prove that the method is true? Whatever technique we employ to prove that the method is true needs now to be proven to be true. So how do you prove the "prover"? You can't.

Those who believe in the Scientific Method are still building their belief upon faith! "I have faith in my senses. I have faith in my rationality. I have faith in this method, but I can't prove the method to be true." The Scientific Method is a philosophy. The Scientific Method is a good method for ascertaining data and learning about our world, but it doesn't absolutely prove anything.

So if you were asked, "Which of the following is based on faith: philosophy, chemistry, physics, psychology, sociology, science, or theology?" what would be the correct answer? The answer is all of the above. They are all based on faith. Everything is based on faith. (We are talking at a presupposition level.)

If we accept the Scientific Method as a good method, then we seek "facts" that are testable, measurable. We want to make observations and weed out old ideas. It is a good method; but one of the drawbacks of the Scientific Method is that it is only good for that which is observable. When we consider subjects such as angels or the existence of God, the Scientific Method doesn't help us much with our analysis and our study.

So what do we do with that?[31]

SUMMARY OF "FACTS, NOT FAITH"

"Facts, not Faith" is not a valid concept, first, because it is not "integrating" psychology and theology at all and, secondly, because there are NO real "facts" (in the absolute sense). There is faith in what we believe to be facts. "I have faith in my facts." But faith is the key element to all of the "facts."

2. The Word, Not World Wisdom

ELIMINATE PSYCHOLOGY

The second view says, "No, no, 'It's the Word, not Worldly Wisdom.' Psychology is of the world. It's worldly wisdom. Let's throw that out."

It is apparent that neither this view nor the previous one is really a view of integration. Those who hold to the first two views look at psychology and theology and discard one of them. In the first view, they eliminated theology entirely. In this view, psychology is eliminated entirely.

Those who advocate this view say, "It's all about the Bible." "The only wisdom that can be found is in the Bible." "The only way to understand our thinking and beliefs is through studying the Bible."

Now, what's wrong with that? That doesn't sound like a bad view does it? Don't we want the Bible to be the core of our thinking? Certainly! The Bible is the basis for the Christian life. So what could possibly be wrong with this view from the Christian perspective?

Proponents of this view suggest that psychology was built upon a humanistic philosophy or "Secular Humanism." Today the philosophy that

---

[31] Again, this author would like to reiterate that he believes in absolute truth, but as was stated earlier, he *believes* it, but cannot absolutely prove it. What is BELIEVED can be true, yet cannot always be *proven* scientifically here on earth.

is in vogue is termed "Post-Modernism." Given that theology is built upon God's word and not a secular philosophy, those holding this view therefore reject psychology.

As a result of this pairing of psychology with humanistic philosophy, the Christian psychologist is then confronted by advocates of this view with inquiries such as, "How can you be a psychologist and be a Christian?" In the mind of many who are supporters of this view, psychology is "of Satan" and "evil," and theology is of God. Their biggest question is: "How can you put these two together?"

Obviously, if they presuppose those two opposing ideas of Satan versus God, then their questions are very legitimate. This was discussed earlier in this chapter and also in the chapter entitled, "Presuppositions." You *cannot* put those two opposing views together.

Others who hold to this view have said, "Moses and Paul -- did they need psychology? Why do WE need psychology?"

What is the answer to those questions? Did Moses need psychology? Did Paul need psychology? Why is it that, today, we "need" psychology?

ONE EXAMPLE OF PSYCHOLOGY IN THE BIBLE
-- JETHRO COUNSELS MOSES

Take a look at Exodus 18. Jethro, Moses' father-in-law, came for a visit at the time that Moses was leading the nation of Israel. The day following the first day's greetings, Moses went to work while his father-in-law looked on.

As Jethro was observing Moses, he noted that Moses was not applying the best plan as he cared for the people's problems. Jethro realized that Moses' *behavior* was not going to be helpful to his own well-being. Moses was not *thinking* correctly when it came to addressing so many people's problems. So Jethro *counseled* Moses concerning his flawed approach.

Jethro said to Moses (in essence), "What you're doing is not smart." He said, "Why are you trying to do all this alone? . . . This is not good! You're going to wear yourself out -- and the people too." He then counseled Moses to get help, having other honest and capable men handle the little problems and Moses handle the most difficult ones. "That will make your load lighter, because they will share it with you. If you do this and God so commands, you will be able to stand the strain, and all these people will go home satisfied," he concluded (Ex. 18:23).

First of all, that's counseling. That's psychology. Secondly, Jethro is

---

³² Jethro/Moses picture (Item: #692777) purchased from clipart.com, 2/1/11.

counseling Moses to apply "self-care" or "self-management." That's psychology. It's in there.

As a Christian, challenge yourself while reading the Bible to search for the places where that kind of psychology is present. You may be amazed to find how much psychology is there.

Now here is an important point to consider. Could application of such psychological principles help those Christians who go too far with their need to be spiritual and/or push other Christians to overwork for the apparent sake of godliness? Could psychology such as this point out the fallacies of those who say, "Hey, burn out for God!" "Just keep working and if you burn out, at least you burn out doing the right thing."

Why didn't Jethro say that? Wouldn't that sound more spiritual? Many Christians think that if you are going to burn out, "Burn out for God and don't worry about taking care of yourself," or "Just go out there and be a martyr. Do whatever people ask of you."

But Jethro applied psychology by observing what was happening (the detriment that Moses was potentially doing to himself) and counseling Moses to change his approach. Jethro wanted Moses to be able to preserve his ability to be useful. He suggested that Moses *think* differently about how he was going about his work and encouraged him to *change his behavior.* That is what is often missed by those who don't think that psychology and the Bible can be together. The stories of the Bible have psychology woven all through them.

So those who propose the idea that Moses and others didn't need psychology are missing something. How are they defining psychology? Are they some of the ones who are saying that "Psychology equals Freud, Skinner, and Rogers"? That is an important distinction to be made and realized about those who adamantly oppose psychology. Sometimes what they are against is *not* the essence of psychology. It is an *aspect* of psychology.

SUMMARY OF "THE WORD, NOT WORLDLY WISDOM"

Psychology is *not* Freud, Skinner, and Rogers. Psychology didn't begin in 1879 with Wilhelm Wundt, who set up the first "laboratory" for psychology and began putting the focus on some of the more scientific aspects of psychology. (He pioneered the *science* of psychology, not psychology itself.) Psychology (thinking/the mind and behavior) has been around forever. It didn't start with Wundt or Freud. Thinking and behavior and decisions made to influence or react to thinking and behavior have been a part of man's world since creation.

So, psychology is *not* Freud, Skinner, and Rogers; it *is* the study of mind and behavior, period! The Bible has a lot to say about the human mind and behavior.

3. Accept Both, Integrate Neither

The third view is not really a view of integration either because it declares: "Both of them are good. Let's keep both. But don't try to bring them together."

There are Christian people and Christian schools that believe that the disciplines of theology and psychology are totally separate and should not be brought together and, yet, both are useful. In some schools, the two disciplines are housed in totally separate buildings with rare interaction. There is a deliberate intention NOT to bring them together. Those who hold this view of "integration" are convinced that this is the best way to approach the subject, and it would be unwise, otherwise, to bring them together. This view is held with conviction by some godly Christians. "Accept Both, Integrate Neither" assumes that both are equally valid and, yet, should not be integrated.

So is this the best approach -- that we shouldn't try to bring the two disciplines together? Is it true that there is NO overlap at all? If not, how does one keep them separate?

HOW DO YOU PUT PROBLEMS IN A CAMP?

Consider the psychological manifestation of anxiety. Everyone has anxiety from time to time -- all people! None of us are exempt from worry or concern about something. Whether Christians or non-Christians, we are all bombarded with things that can consume our thoughts.

So, in theology, can it be said that the topic of anxiety does not come up? What about "Do not be anxious about anything, but in everything, by prayer and petition, with thanksgiving, present your requests to God" (Phil. 4:6) or "Do not worry about tomorrow" (Matt. 6:34)? So the question then is: "Is anxiety a spiritual problem or a psychological problem?"

Do you see the dilemma? How do you put anxiety in a camp?

"Well, if I'm worried about spiritual things, then it is a spiritual problem and if I am having anxiety about my world, then is it a psychological problem." Is that a good distinction?

"When I'm not really trusting God, I get anxious." According to the above explanation, it sounds like that is a spiritual problem. The Bible says not to be anxious about anything.

But, if I am having panic attacks, then that must be a psychological problem? -- Not a spiritual problem? How do you separate the psychological aspect of anxiety from the spiritual aspect? How do you discuss the inclination that anyone has (including Christians) to worry or be concerned, without viewing the *thinking* that is behind the emotion or activity and using a *biblical* approach to determine the cause and treatment?

What about "fear"? Why were the shepherds afraid when the angels came to them (Luke 2:8-9)? What was going on inside them?

Or why did the angels think that their announcement would bring the shepherds joy (Luke 2:10-20)? Joy is another emotion. How could the angels anticipate that emotion? Are those spiritual feelings or psychological feelings? Are they spiritual because angels are involved?

What if I am afraid to fly? Is that a psychological problem because it concerns aircraft, or is it a spiritual problem because I am not trusting God?

UNWARRANTED DISTINCTION

Another problem with this approach is that many times, in order to promote this way of thinking, an unwarranted distinction is created between soul and spirit. Those who make this kind of distinction between soul and spirit might say, "If you have a psychological problem, you should see your psychologist. If you have a spiritual problem, you should visit your pastor."

So, if you have an anxiety problem, whom do you go to see? Can you make that kind of distinction? -- Probably not. AND, as will be discussed later in this book, it is doubtful that that kind of distinction can be made *theologically* either.

How about depression? Is that a spiritual problem? Marital problems -- are they spiritual or psychological? There is probably not a line where one can say that it is one or the other.

Some people have said, "Psychology has more to do with people on earth and theology has more to do with heaven." Some thought-provoking points could be made in that regard, but that kind of hard distinction cannot be supported by the biblical data.

There are those who do try to categorize such previously mentioned problems and make clear distinctions that cause tremendous damage because they try to guide people without a proper understanding of all of the inner-workings and complexities of those problems. They may use wrong Scriptures to try to help because they misunderstand what is wrong. Or they may use improper techniques because they do not understand the spiritual depth of the difficulty being presented and/or the ramifications of their techniques and advice.

SUMMARY OF "ACCEPT BOTH, INTEGRATE NEITHER"

So, to summarize this section, a hard and fast designation that "This is your 'psyche' or your 'psychological part,' which is distinct from your 'spiritual part,'" does not exist. It is therefore the conclusion of this writer that using a trichotomist view to separate the psychological and the theological/spiritual part is not a proper approach to viewing the problems that confront man. No clear chart can be drawn to specify one problem as being totally psychological and another problem as being totally spiritual.

FRANCIS BACON
From a painting

4. The Two-Book View

We will now move to the most common view of integration -- the "Two-Book View." In most Christian circles, when the topic of integrating psychology and theology is discussed, this view tends to represent what is endorsed.

The two-book view was originated by the philosopher, Francis Bacon, in the 17th century, who believed that there were two types of revelation: the Bible -- "Special Revelation" and the created universe -- "General Revelation."[33] Bacon wanted to give credence to scientific study among the religious world. [34] [35]

---

[33] Andrew S. Kulikovsky, "Scripture and General Revelation," *Journal of Creation* 19, no.2 (2005): 23-28

[34] Some information gathered in this section is from an article on the Internet by John C. Hutchinson in March 1998 from the *Journal of the Evangelical Theological Society*. The Internet article is entitled "The Design Argument in Scientific Discourse: Historical-Theological Perspective from the Seventeenth Century." http://74.125.95.132/search?q=cache:IJW8x-gVBrkJ:findarticles.com/p/articles/mi_qa3817/is_199803/ai_n8790594+John+C.+Hutchinson+in+March+1998+from+the+Journal+of+the+Evangelical+Theological+Society.The+Design+Argument+in+Scientific+Discourse:&cd=1&hl=en&ct=clnk&gl=us

[35] Photo of Francis Bacon from http://www.ourenglish.org/huanghaoshu.html. Photo in Public Domain.

The idea was renewed in the 1970s by Kirk Farnsworth, who included psychology under the heading of "General Revelation" (what God has given the world).[36] "General Revelation," in this view, includes scientific study through empiricism and observation. The goal is to find out, through science, what is true in the world. (Psychology -- especially scientific psychology -- would be a part of that.) General Revelation assumes that there is truth to be found in the world that God has revealed because God has made a world that has truth in it.

The second "book" of the Two-Book View involves "Special Revelation." Special Revelation is where the Bible is the central focus. Hermeneutics -- or how you interpret the Bible -- is an important part of that study. The languages of the Bible -- primarily Greek and Hebrew -- are also an important part of that "Special Revelation." From those and other aspects of study, one develops his "theology."

---

[36] Kirk E. Farnsworth, "Psychology and Christianity: A Substantial Integration, " *Journal of the American Scientific Affiliation, Science in Christian Perspective*, JASA27 (June 1975): 60-66. An expanded version of this paper was presented at the 1974 Convention of the Christian Association for Papeholoeial Studies and was published in the *Journal of Psychology and Theology* 2, 116-124 (1974).

The Two-Book View

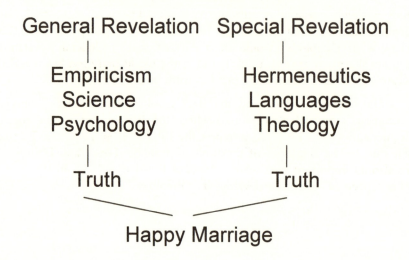

General Revelation   Special Revelation
| |
Empiricism   Hermeneutics
Science   Languages
Psychology   Theology
| |
Truth   Truth

Happy Marriage

[37]

So the goal is to put together the truths of General Revelation and the truths of Special Revelation. It is assumed that if the two are put together, then there will be a "happy marriage." Now, what could be wrong with that?

It makes a nice chart, but is it biblical? What do we do if those who interpret the truths don't agree? The real world is not always so neatly divided. And who is making the decisions on what the "truths" are and how are those decisions being made? On what are those decisions based?

PROBLEM #1 -- WHAT IF THEY DON'T AGREE?

When they don't agree, what typically happens is that those who hold to this view tend to "fall off" on the scientific side. The thinking goes something like this: "Well, the Bible was written 2,000 years ago and we know a lot more now. We have more and better data."

This is especially true with topics like homosexuality. "Well, that was

---

[37] Chart is author's interpretation of information given in a Chart found in *Understanding People* by Lawrence J. Crabb, Jr. (Winona Lake, IN: BMH Books, 1987), 38.

written by Paul. We know today that his view is not right and, therefore, we have to look at homosexuality from a different vantage point."

So, the question then becomes, "What do you mean we know Paul is not right?" How do we know that Paul is not right?

The problem with the "Two-Book View" is that if there is a discrepancy and there is indecision as to which "book" to go with, then, all of a sudden, the Bible tends to get "explained away" with the assertion that man is much more knowledgeable now than he was 2,000 years ago. Shouldn't that make Christians a little nervous? Didn't God give us a more solid foundation than that one -- that wavers and is adjusted through time?

C.S. Lewis wrote of "Chronological Snobbery" -- "the uncritical acceptance of the intellectual climate common to our own age and the assumption that whatever has gone out of date is on that account discredited."[38] The idea is that "our" generation is the "smart bunch." Are we really smarter than those whom God ordained to pen the words of Scripture? Or are we now putting ourselves above God? Christians need to take a careful look at the implications of this type of thinking.

Isaiah 55:8-9 says, "For my thoughts are not your thoughts, neither are your ways my ways . . . my ways (are) higher than your ways and my thoughts (are higher) than your thoughts."

Proverbs 3:5 says, "Trust in the Lord with all your heart and lean not on your own understanding."

God is trying to communicate to us that our minds are never fully able to comprehend Him and His world. We must rely on Him and His word to give us the only enduring truths that are to be known. To rely on our own wisdom apart from God and His word is foolishness.

PROBLEM #2 -- THEY HAVE DIFFERENT PURPOSES

The next problem: What is the purpose of each one? What is the purpose of General Revelation? What is the purpose of Special Revelation? Take a look at the two passages regarding General and Special Revelation in this section.

---

[38] C. S. Lewis, *Surprised by Joy* (New York: Harcourt, Inc., 1955), 207-208.

General Revelation:[39]

Psalm 19:1 – The *heavens* declare the glory of God;
the skies proclaim the work of his hands.

The Bible tells us that the creations of God demonstrated in our world (General Revelation), declare God and His glory. If that is true, when we observe or study anything in the world, including psychology, we are saying, "Wow, look at God! Look at what He made. This is incredible!"

But, the purpose of General Revelation was not necessarily to teach me how to live life. The purpose was not to help me with my marriage or to learn how to love my roommate or my sibling better. When I go out at night and look at the stars, I don't come back in and say, "I think I know what I need to do now." When I spend time with the trees, I don't say, "You know what? I think this has really helped my morality."

It does tell me: "Look at God!! He's an awesome God. He's an incredible God. He's the One to worship."

When we study the intricacies of our world, we see that they reveal a lot about Him. But is that study going to tell me how to live a fulfilling and moral life? -- Probably not.

The purpose of Special Revelation is quite different from that of General Revelation. "All Scripture is God-breathed and profitable for teaching, rebuking, correcting, and training in righteousness" (2 Tim. 3:16). When I go to God's word -- "Special Revelation" -- I find principles to live my life by. I find the answers to the way I need to think and what I need to do. I find a reason for my existence.

---

[39]Photo from http://publicdomainclip-art.blogspot.com/2006/07/space-final-frontier-andromeda-galaxy.html.. A guide to better quality more plentiful public domain royalty free copyright free high resolution images, stock photos, jpgs and clipart free for commercial use.

So to put them (Psychology/General Revelation and Theology/Special Revelation) on the same level and say they are equal in terms of purpose does not seem to fit God's intention. Although the stars and trees and plant life certainly declare God's glory and tell a lot about Him, they fall short of giving us what we need to know in order to "find God, know God, and serve God." The difference in purposes is important to consider because God's creation is not intended to be a "teacher" of morality, only a demonstrator of an awesome God!

PROBLEM #3 -- CLARITY

And yet another problem exists: What is the clarity of each? How clear is General Revelation in terms of how we are to live our lives? We have already concluded that General Revelation is not very clear when it comes to morality and living life.

When looking at Special Revelation, Scripture is clear in some cases and unclear in others. Of those instances where Scripture is not as clear, a study of our world can help try to discover what God intended. But one problem that often surfaces with many conservative, fundamentalistic Christians, is an intentional "forcing of clarity" where clarity is not found. There is a tendency to twist the intended message and follow the idea that, "Where the Scripture is clear, be clear; where Scripture is vague, be clear; and where Scripture is silent, be clear." Those who feel that specific answers are always there to be found in Scripture, often "force" those specific answers for problems when they are not given -- where only "parameters" are given. "Manufacturing" answers to promote clarity in Scripture does not seem be what God intended when those Scriptures were penned.

Does the Bible say anything about Multiple Personality Disorder (renamed Dissociative Identity Disorder)? A person once insisted to this author, "Yeah. It has to, because that disorder is out there. If it exists, then the Bible HAS to say something about it." Does it?

The following "proof" was given: "The double-minded man is unstable in all his ways" (James 1:8). Is that verse talking about Multiple Personality Disorder? It is improbable that James is talking about Multiple Personality Disorder when it refers to a "double-minded man."

How about Nebuchadnezzar grazing in the pasture (Dan. 4:28-33)?

Well, that was God's curse on him, but would you call that Schizophrenia? Does the Bible really tell us about Schizophrenia? Not really. There is no clear reference to Schizophrenia or Multiple Personality Disorder in the Bible. We need to be very careful when we make proclamations about biblical clarity that may not really be there.

Sometimes Christian speakers will declare that Multiple Personality Disorder/Dissociative Identity Disorder equals demon possession. As Christians, we should cautiously evaluate such assertions. There is no scriptural evidence to support the idea that Multiple Personality Disorder is demon possession.

Could there be spiritual influences? -- Absolutely. But there could also be spiritual influences in the very room where you sit as you read this book. There could be spiritual influences present with depression and anxiety. Negative spiritual influences or demonic influences may even affect people who look spiritual and well put-together.

How do we know that to be true? The Pharisees looked great. But, in speaking to them, Christ made reference to "Your father, the devil" (John 8:44). So even those that look pretty good -- pretty "spiritual" – to us, can have demonic influences affecting their lives.

We need to be very careful when we make proclamations about biblical clarity that may not really be there. The Bible does not speak specifically to every life event, issue, or circumstance; nor does our world teach us the correct view of morality and godly living.

PROBLEM #4 -- ON THE SAME LEVEL?

40

Since General Revelation and Special Revelation have different purposes and because there is a difference in clarity, it would be erroneous to see them as being on the same plane or on the same level. If one of the revelation types were to be put above the other, then it would seem that Special Revelation would be viewed as more important and the grid through which all other information should be processed. General Revelation would then be positioned below Special Revelation. If an error were to be made, it would seem to be "safer" to err on the side of evaluating everything through Scripture than to leave those important evaluations to human assessments. Though General Revelation is helpful to us (especially in the "hard" sciences such as Biology and Chemistry), it is limited when it comes to things like morality, spirituality, angels, God, right, and wrong.

SUMMARY OF THE TWO-BOOK VIEW

Though putting the two types of revelation together seems like a good system in theory, the view brings dilemmas regarding agreement, differences in purpose, clarity, and inequality.

---

[40]Scale image from clker.com found at http://www.clker.com/clipart-11097.html. "Settlement Law Justice" shared by Mohamed Ibrahim. This is a free image in the public domain.

---

5. Scriptural Foundation, Secular Nuggets

INTRODUCTION – 4 DEFINITIONS OF PSYCHOLOGY

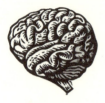  

Take a look again now at the question that is under consideration: "Does psychology have anything good to offer?" Before answering that question, our terms must be defined. We have previously concluded that the accepted definition of psychology used in this book is "the study of mind and behavior," and all that that entails. It was noted how faulty presuppositions -- "underlying beliefs"[41] -- can affect one's viewpoint. But consider now a more in-depth look at a few of the popular definitions of psychology.

Though there are many definitions of psychology floating around in various circles, four will be examined here: 1) **The Study of Mind and Behavior.** 2) **The "Scientific" Study of Mind**[42] **and Behavior.** 3) **The Study of the "Soul" (psuche) in Scripture.**[43] 4) **Theories of Psychology such as those of Freud, Skinner, and Rogers.**[44]

The first definition is more of a philosophy: "Let's look at mind and behavior and theorize about them." The second one is saying, "No, let's conduct some experiments and make some scientific observations in order to figure out what this entity is all about." The third refers to the study of the "soul" in the Bible. (The term "psuche" – psyche, which is the Greek term for "soul" -- or sometimes translated "heart" -- is studied. This word is different from "pneuma" -- spirit.) And the fourth definition revolves around the theories of psychologists, such as: Freud, Skinner, and Rogers.

---

[41] Refer to page 38 of this document.

[42] Brain image from MicrosoftWord7 Clip Art.

[43] Book image from MicrosoftWord7 Clip Art.

[44] Image of Sigmund Freud -- BING image public domain, Sigmund Freud

So to answer the question: "Does psychology have anything good to offer?" we have to first ask: "What do you mean by 'psychology'?" Which of those four are we talking about?

1) THE STUDY OF MIND AND BEHAVIOR

If you are a believer in the first definition, then you accept that psychology is "**The Study of Mental and Behavioral Processes.**" Here, psychology is simply a neutral term. It is *not* sinful. It is like Biology, Chemistry, and Physics. It is simply a term denoting the *study* of something -- mind and behavior. And the study of something isn't sinful.

Now, one's conclusions could be sinful. The results could differ from what God wants. But the study of something is neutral. And it has been stated previously in this book: psychology reflects God, just like all of the other subjects reflect God. Math reflects God. Biology reflects God. Chemistry reflects God . . . Philosophy . . . Physics. They all reflect God. He is the inventor of them. And anything that reflects God is worth studying. "Great are the works of the Lord; They are studied by all who delight in them," says Psalm 111:2 (KJV).

2) THE "SCIENTIFIC" STUDY OF MIND AND BEHAVIOR

What about the "**Scientific**" **Study of Mental and Behavioral Processes?** Could adding the scientific component make it bad? Well, science is neutral. That has already been discussed. Simply bringing things through our senses and trying to make sense of them is a philosophical way of finding truth, and that is also neutral. So you have "neutral" on top of "neutral" -- nothing sinful yet.

In fact, science is biblical. What does Genesis 1:28 say? What are we supposed to do with our world? We are to subdue it and have dominion over it as a representation of God here on the Earth. How can that be done without studying it? How do I subdue anything and have dominion over it without studying it, knowing it, and understanding how it functions best? So science is biblical. Psychology is biblical.

But science, as important as it is, is limited. It is helpful for that which is "immanent." Science is not so helpful for that which is "transcendent." We are back to that presupposition again.

So science is limited to that which is immanent -- the stuff that I can see, the created domain. Science is very helpful for those things. We are very thankful for the medical community and what it has found for us, but it is limited.

It cannot help much with that which is transcendent. Science will not and cannot prove God. Science will not prove that there are angels. Science will not prove that there is a heaven or hell or demonic forces. It doesn't have the capability to do that.

Now, one day, we will all be good scientists. How do we know that? The Bible says that one day every tongue will confess and every knee shall bow (Phil. 2:10) and we will all be good empiricists and say, "There He is." Every tongue! Every knee! Everyone will say: "There is a God and I now believe." Why? "I see it." One day, we will all be empiricists. On this side of heaven, however, we have to take things by faith.

In his book, *Disappointment with God*, Philip Yancey shares an analogy told by C. S. Lewis regarding a beam of light[45] in a dark tool shed. He says, "When he first entered the shed, he saw a beam and looked at the luminous band of brightness filled with floating specks of dust.

45Title: "Dark Room With Spotlight," © Miguel Mariano Pagella purchased from dreamstime.com 1/27/11.

But, when he moved over to the beam and looked *along* it, he gained a very different perspective. Suddenly, he saw, not the beam, but framed in the window of the shed, green leaves,[46] moving on the branches of a tree outside and beyond that, 93 million miles away, the sun. Looking *at* the beam and looking *along* the beam are quite different."[47]

What is the point? Science is an effective instrument for studying the beam. You can measure how long the beam is. You can count how many specks of dust there are in the beam. You can study what the light is made up of and note that light, itself, is made up of particles (photons). You can observe the contrast of the beam of light to the darkness -- which is simply the absence of light. However, science cannot look *along* the beam -- through it -- to the source beyond. It can't tell us the source of the beam. It can't tell us what is out there. Faith is required to look along the beam. Science is a tremendous instrument for looking at the beam; however, science is limited.

---

[46] Light rays picture purchased from dreamstime.com. © Ivan Pheoktistov. Title: "Sunbeam." Accessed 1/27/11.

[47] Philip Yancey, *Disappointment with God* (Grand Rapids: Zondervan, 1988), 218.

3) THE STUDY OF THE "SOUL" (PSUCHE) IN SCRIPTURE

How about the study of the soul, "psuche," in Scripture? God created mental and behavioral processes; therefore, those processes reflect God. The word "soul," or "psuche," is often used in Scripture to describe those deep inner-workings of man's beliefs and thinking. The important point to remember when looking at the idea of integrating psychology and theology (which was stated earlier in this chapter) is: Psychology is inherent in the Bible message. There is an inherent psychology in our theology.

When we study the Greek word "psuche"[48] or "soul" (and sometimes translated "heart") in Scripture, we see a wealth of psychology. In fact, that word alone sheds light on the makeup of man, dealing with all of his thoughts, emotions, and what drives his behaviors.

Proverbs 23:7 ". . . as he thinketh in his heart/soul (translated in NASB "within himself"), so is he" (KJV). In the secular approach of Cognitive Therapy, thinking is vitally important to understanding the person and the Cognitive Therapist bases his theory on that truth. But understanding the "soul" seems to be stressed in biblical references for the Christian as well, and this psychology is part of our theology.

Two Greek words make up our word psychology: "psuche' " -- psych, and "logos" -- ology. "Psuche" is the Greek word for "soul." When we study the soul and see how it is referred to in Scripture, we are learning about how man is made up -- how he thinks and how that thinking is the basis for his behavior. My soul or mind is the center for my thinking, action, emotions, etc.

---

[48] "Psuche" is also discussed in chapter 3.

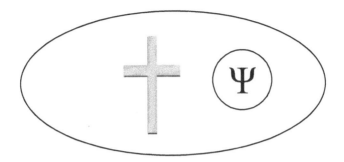

The large oval that surrounds the cross in the above diagram[49] represents theology and psychology is represented by the encircled Greek symbol, "Ψ."[50] The diagram illustrates the point that inside of our theology is a psychology. There is a study of behavioral and mental processes in our theology. God made our minds which dictate our behaviors and they are part of our theology. A person's mental state (thinking) and the behaviors that emerge based from that thinking are discussed in the Bible. So any time someone looks into Scripture and finds the word "mind" or behavior, or how people emoted, or the word "soul" and then processes what is being communicated in that passage, that person is discovering something about theology. That "psychology" is part of our "theology."

Our theology is not a sterile thing. Our theology does not consist of simply knowing the five points of Calvinism. That is *part* of theology; but, that is not the full embodiment of our theology. Our theology is demonstrated in the way we treat people. The way we behave toward others is theology. Did God have anything to say about how we treat people? Yes!

---

[49] Diagram by author, Thomas J. Edgington, Ph.D.

[50] Let me add a subpoint while on this topic. Psychology can be symbolized by the Greek letter "psy" --Ψ. There are people who have said, "Ah, that's the devil's pitchfork!" There are a couple of problems with that. Number one, it is the Greek letter, not a pitchfork. It is neutral. The same letter is used in many other words that could not even be "stretched" to mean something evil. To put that kind of pronouncement upon the letter, just because it is the beginning of the word "psychology," seems a bit forced.   Secondly, the Devil doesn't have a pitchfork. He's not red and he does not have a big long tail. That is *not* Satan.

Our theology begins with our thinking and is demonstrated by how we live our lives. And yet, many find themselves sometimes believing, "Yeah, well that's the *practical* side, but actually *studying theology* is better."

No! The way we treat people *is* theology! In fact, it is a pretty important part of our theology. The way we hold our theology is as much theology as the theology to which we hold. Both are vital!

The study of the word "soul" alone provides much evidence of that deep inner part of man -- the part that consists of the beliefs that influence how we think and how we live our lives. And when the evidences of the word "soul" are combined with the remaining teachings of the Bible, we find even more material that enlightens us and instructs our thinking and behavior. The entire Bible contains a wealth of material for the field of psychology.

4) THEORIES OF PSYCHOLOGY SUCH AS THOSE OF FREUD, SKINNER, AND ROGERS

The last definition that some attribute to psychology is that psychology consists of the theories of famous psychologists such as Sigmund Freud, B. F. Skinner, and Carl Rogers.

51

52

53

[51] Sigmund Freud photograph 1938, Public Domain image. http://psychology.about.com/od/historyofpsychology/ig/Pictures-of-Psychologists/Sigmund-Freud-Picture.htm. Also http://www.wpclipart.com/famous/psychology/Sigmund_Freud.png.html. Images are all in the Public Domain and may be used for commercial as well as personal projects, royalty free. (A link is appreciated but not necessary.)

[52] B. F. Skinner, psychologist. This picture is from PsychArt, a public domain library of famous psychologists. http://www.sonoma.edu/psychology/psychart.htm

Though they were psychologists that contributed to the field of psychology, they were men who held wrong presuppositions. Therefore, aspects of their theories are wrong. Obviously, they didn't believe that, but many of their presuppositions contradict biblical teachings. And what is interesting about each of their theories is that all of them reacted against religion on some level.

Sigmund Freud was raised by Jewish parents while living in the Roman Catholic town of Freiburg, Moravia. He wrote a number of books interpreting the religious influences he encountered.[54] "Religion is comparable to a childhood neurosis," he wrote in *The Future of an Illusion*.[55] "The different religions have never overlooked the part played by the sense of guilt in civilization. What is more, they come forward with a claim...to save mankind from this sense of guilt, which they call sin,"[56] was written in *Civilization and Its Discontents*.

Burrhus Frederic "B. F." Skinner attended a Protestant Sunday School as a child. As a man, he contemplated the ideas he had been taught, which included the fear he had acquired of Hell -- enhanced by his grandmother's warning that children who told lies would go there. He felt that religion had negatively influenced his behavior, causing him to withdraw from others because of his shame over his sexual desires.[57]

After trying religion, he seemed to come to the conclusion that it was a type of crutch that people needed to control behavior and explain baffling situations. "Physics and biology soon abandoned explanations of this sort," he said, "and turned to more useful kinds of causes, but the step has not been decisively taken in the field of human behavior."[58] When

---

[53] Public domain image.
http://psychology.about.com/od/historyofpsychology/ig/Pictures-of-Psychologists/Carl-Rogers-Picture.htm

[54] Books directed toward religion included *Totem and Taboo* (Mineola, New York: Dover Publications, Inc., 1913), *The Future of an Illusion* (London: Hogarth Press, 1927), *Civilization and Its Discontents* (London: Hogarth Press, 1930), and *Moses and Monotheism* (1938).

[55] Sigmund Freud, *The Future of an Illusion*, p. 53.

[56] Freud, *Civilization and Its Discontents* (London: Penguin, 2002) p. 82-83).

[57] Burrhus Frederic Skinner, *Particulars of My Life* (New York: Alfred A. *Knopf, Inc., 1976), p. 110.*

[58] B.F. Skinner, *Beyond Freedom and Dignity* (Indianapolis: Hackett Publishing Company, Inc., 2002), p. 7.

speaking of those who believe in "indwelling agents," he stated, "Although physics soon stopped personifying things in this way, it continued for a long time to speak as if they (people) had wills, impulses, feelings, purposes, and other fragmentary attributes of an indwelling agent. . . . Careless references to purpose are still to be found in both physics and biology, but good practice has no place for them."[59]

Carl Rogers came from a fundamentalist background. Two beliefs that he was taught very strongly at home when he was growing up, were: 1) People are depraved and 2) Do not mix with worldly people.[60]

But, as a psychologist, two of his main tenets could be summarized as: "People are basically good"[61] and "If we all get together, good things will happen." (He was a strong proponent of group counseling/"encounter" groups).[62] He, very much, reacted against some of his religious upbringing even going so far as to say, "Neither the Bible nor the prophets -- neither Freud nor research -- neither the revelations of God nor man -- can take precedence over my own direct experience."[63] Yet, even though he asserted presuppositions that were false, or in some cases, fell short of total accuracy, during his years as a psychologist, he *did* stumble on some truth -- due to the common grace of God.

God allowed all three of the previously mentioned psychologists to be brilliant and allowed them to find some truth. A number of those truths are mentioned throughout this book.

So is psychology basically the theories of Freud, Skinners, and

---

[59] Skinner, *Beyond Freedom and Dignity*, p. 8.

[60] Carl Rogers, *On Becoming a Person* (Boston: Houghton Mifflin Company, 1961), p. 5-7.

[61]"Persons have a basically positive direction." Rogers, *On Becoming a Person*, p. 26. "The core of man's nature is essentially positive." Rogers, *On Becoming a Person,* p. 73, and man is basically a "trustworthy organism." Rogers, *Carl Rogers on Personal Power: Inner Strength and its Revolutionary Impact* (New York: Delacorte Press, 1977), p. 7.

[62] "In an intensive group with much freedom and little structure, the individual will gradually feel safe enough to drop some of his defenses and facades; he will relate more directly on a feeling basis (come into a basic encounter) with other members of the group; he will come to understand himself and his relationship to others more accurately; he will change in his personal attitudes and behavior; and he will subsequently relate more effectively to others in his everyday life situation." Carl Rogers, "The Process of the Basic Encounter Group," in K. Roy MacKenzie's, *Classics in Group Psychotherapy* (New York: The Guilford Press, 1992), p. 217.

[63] Rogers, *On Becoming a Person*, p. 24.

Rogers? No. We have already demonstrated that. But did Freud, Skinner, and Rogers make important contributions to psychology? Yes. Can other non-Christians make contributions that can enlighten us in regard to our understanding of our world? Yes.

And we need to remember that all three of the men previously mentioned were image-bearers. Secularists are still image-bearers. They are made in God's image and gifted with rationality, just as Christians are. Non-Christians can be brilliant people who can think deeply and make accurate observations of their world.

SUMMARY OF DEFINITIONS

So which of the four definitions is correct? Well, they all are in some way because they all include an aspect of psychology -- though they are not all complete. The first definition encompasses all of the other three aspects and is the most comprehensive. It will be the one that can be assumed as you read on to the next pages and chapters of this book. So as you read, assume that psychology means, "The Study of Mind and Behavior" and whatever is involved in that study.

WHAT DO WE TAKE FROM PSYCHOLOGY?

All of this leads to the discussion of the fifth view of integration, which is the view that is held by the writer of this book -- "Scriptural Foundation, Secular Nuggets."

What does that mean? It means that secularists *do* have something to offer that can be of value to the Christian.

So we can say that if integration is defined that way, we are integrationists (though not on a presuppositional level -- since the assumed belief is that psychology is inherent in theology and does not need to be integrated). Yes, we are "integrationists" if we are considering whether secularists have something to offer; but NO, we are not "integrationists" on a presuppositional level because the presuppositions are mutually exclusive.

So what we want to look at is: "How do we use some of those truths that secularists have found?" Jay Adams put it very adeptly in his book, *The Christian Counselor's Manual.* In spite of the fact that Adams has been known to have a strong view against psychology (though possibly because his definition of "psychology" is different from the one espoused in this book), even he realizes the importance of some of the contributions of others in the secular world.

He said, "From the vantage point of his biblical foundation, the Christian counselor may take note of, and evaluate, and *reclaim the truth, dimly reflected by the unbeliever* so long as he does so in a manner that is consistent with biblical principles and methodology."[64] What Adams was saying is that there *is* truth out there that is available to be reclaimed by the Christian. But most importantly, the reclaiming process is preempted by a strong biblical base through which the believer evaluates that truth.

Adams further stated: "On our foundation of biblical presuppositions, there must be built a fuller methodology that grows out of them and that is appropriate to them at every point. The methodology must be oriented biblically and remain in the framework of scriptural principles. When you have constructed a platform like that, then you are able to stand upon it. . ." (That's your foundation.) ". . . look around at what is happening elsewhere, and you can pick and choose and adapt from that perspective, whatever *nuggets* that an unbeliever (in the common grace of God) has unearthed."[65]

---

[64]Jay E. Adams, *The Christian Counselor's Manual* (Phillisburg, New Jersey: Presbyterian and Reformed Publishing Company 1973), 92.

[65] Adams, *The Christian Counselor's Manual,* 93.

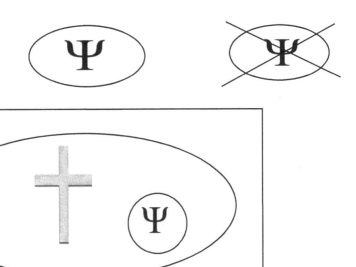

Yes! There is our foundation. Our theology is our foundation. Yet, within that theology, is a psychology. We don't have to integrate that. It is already *in* our theology. Mind, behavior, how we treat people, relationships, marriage, depression, anxiety -- they are all there. But once we have that foundation, then we can build upon it.

In the secular world, we can pick and choose and adapt what secularists have unearthed. They stumbled upon it. God let them have brilliant minds. As Christians, let's reclaim the information that they discovered through His enlightenment, for His glory. Let's use that!! Let's make use of the good information! Now if the ideas are *not* on that biblical foundation, then let's discard them.

So it all boils down to this: Accept what is complementary. Reject what is contradictory.

Accept what is complementary -- what complements Scripture. But if it doesn't complement Scripture, if it is saying that Scripture is wrong, let's reject that. Let's throw that out!

EXAMPLES OF HELPFUL NUGGETS

So what are some examples of helpful nuggets?[66] Some question this view of integration; they want to know what contributions psychology can make that would be helpful to the Christian. The following are examples of helpful nuggets.

Example 1

What's the best mechanism to lessen prejudice? In 1954, Gordon Allport wrote a book entitled *The Nature of Prejudice* which espoused the "Contact Hypothesis."[67] He said that *under certain conditions*, direct contact between members of opposing groups would reduce prejudice. (The conditions were important since just putting them together could actually increase prejudice, as one study showed.)[68] The conditions were: equal status, no competition, contact being sanctioned by authority, and common goals (also known as "superordinate goals").

---

[66] Photo purchased from dreamstime.com. ID: 10135122 Level: Size: 3,886 KB (12.7 MP) © Otnaydur **"Breakthrough wall holding gold nuggets."** Royalty Free images can be used. Worldwide rights/unlimited projects up to 500,000 printed copies (unlimited online).

[67]Gordon Allport, *The Nature of Prejudice* (Cambridge, Massachusetts: Addison-Wesley Publishing Co., Inc., 1954).

[68] Walter Stephan, "The Effects of School Desegregation: an Evaluation 30 Years after Brown," M. J. Saks and L. Saxe (eds) *Advances in Applied Social Psychology*, 3 (1986) 181-206 (Hillsdale NJ: Erlbaum).

The movie, *Remember the Titans*,[69] is a great example of common or "superordinate goals." The football players were not simply combined. The two prejudiced sides were put together with a common goal. As was shown in the movie, when two sides are joined with a cooperative goal that they have to work together to meet, the prejudice dissipates.

Now, is that in the Bible? No, not directly. But the Bible does tell us not to be prejudiced and not to lift one above another. We shouldn't give the best seat to the rich and cast aside the poor (James 2:1-4). The Bible gives us parameters.

So some people who do not claim to be Christians have discovered things that are very useful in terms of what will help reduce prejudice. Though traditional teaching or preaching can be effective, other methods can sometimes teach lessons even better.

Example 2

Another example involves studies that were conducted to discover better ways to help girls learn math. Anita Li and Georgina Adamson found that the type of classroom environment affected girls' interest. The idea of competitiveness seemed to be a hindrance to girls' enthusiasm and thus their learning of math.[70] Judy Diamond and Deborah Bono also found gender differences, each claiming that cooperative environments (group learning) were helpful to girls learning math.[71]

What do you think? In a typical math class, what happens? A typical math class is visual -- diagrams are put on the board. And how are

---

[69] *Remember the Titans*, Directed by Boaz Yakin (Produced by Jerry Bruckheimer for Walt Disney Pictures: 2000).

[70] Anita Li and Georgina Adamson, "Gifted Secondary Students' Preferred Learning Style: Cooperative, Competitive, or Individualistic?" *Journal of Education of the Gifted*, 16, no. 1 (1992), 46-54. http://mathforum.org/~sarah/Discussion.Sessions/biblio.attitudes.html (accessed January 7, 2009).

[71] Judy Diamond, "Sex differences in Science Museums; A Review," *Curator*, 37, no. 1, (March 1994), 17-24. Deborah Bono, "The Impact of Cooperative Learning on Suzy and Janie's Attitudes about Math," Research Report in Virginia (1991). http://mathforum.org/~sarah/Discussion.Sessions/biblio.attitudes.html (accessed January 7, 2009).

students arranged in the classroom? Often, all are in individual seats and work on problems individually. Or sometimes the environment is competitive, where the "fastest" one to figure out the problem is rewarded in some way. So, many times, girls begin to doubt their abilities to learn in that competitive environment. Some have therefore concluded that girls are not very good in math.

What the research has shown is: Girls, who are more relational, tend to learn math better if they can talk about it, sit at tables where they can "process it" with other students, and help each other. They tend not to learn math as well in a competitive environment. Boys learn it a little bit better when they do it by themselves -- more independently or "compete" in some way. Girls can be just as good in math. They just learn it differently.

Nowhere in the Bible does it tell us that girls learn math better in a relational style and boys learn better in an individualistic style, but this is very helpful to know if you are in the teaching profession.

Example 3

The Premack principle is another helpful piece of information that is useful for Christians, yet not found in the Bible. The Premack principle, developed by David Premack, states that a commonly occurring action (one more desirable for the actor) can be used effectively to reinforce a less commonly occurring one (that is, one less desirable for the actor). A common example used to illustrate this principle is a parent requiring a child to clean his or her room before he or she can watch TV. We practiced this in our own home when our children were growing up by allowing dessert only if they ate at least one spoonful of peas or other food they found less desirable. In this case, an activity that probably does not require reinforcement, is used as a reinforcer for cleaning the room or eating vegetables, which in the context of this example the child would not normally choose to do without reinforcement.[72] Again, it is not found in the Bible directly, yet a useful psychological tool.

---

[72] http://psychology.wikia.com/wiki/Premack_principle.

Example 4

What about Fundamentalist Christians? Are they all the same? The intention of the study conducted in 1988 was to show that all fundamentalists are not alike.[73] Researchers in the past have lumped fundamentalists into a single category showing them to be rather simplistic, "black-and-white" thinkers. The attempt was to demonstrate that all fundamentalists are not alike. Some are very complex in their thinking while others are more simplistic. The findings supported the notion that among fundamentalists (those that adhere to certain conservative values), there exists a continuum of fundamentalism with rigidity, defensiveness, and close-mindedness at one end and with more tolerance, less defensiveness, and greater open-mindedness at the other end. All fundamentalists are not alike, as some might want to conclude.

Example 5

A fifth example is of a study conducted by a Christian psychologist -- Dr. Donald Joy. His study looked at the effects of value-oriented instruction in both the church and the home.[74]

Dr. Joy was looking at church class instruction (Sunday School class) vs. parental home instruction to see the effects of both and how they compared to each other. In the midst of his research, he discovered a "serendipitous finding." He found that boys tended to learn better in a nontraditional setting (i.e., a non-classroom setting -- which would be different from Sunday School, which tended to be more of a classroom setting) whereas, girls seemed to do better in the traditional setting.

Some have believed that boys don't learn as well as girls. But it could

---

[73] Thomas James Edgington, *Fundamentalism Viewed as a Single Dimension and Multi-Variately in Predicting a Level of Cognitive Complexity among Fundamentalist Seminary Students* (PhD diss., Ball State University, Muncie, IN, 1988). Also, Thomas J. Edgington and Roger L. Hutchinson, "Fundamentalism as a Predictor of Cognitive Complexity," *Journal of Psychology and Christianity* Vol. 9, No. 1 (Spring, 1990), p. 47.

[74] Donald Joy, *The Effects of Value-Oriented Instruction in the Church and in the Home* (PhD diss., Indiana University, 1969).

be that boys would learn as much as girls if they were are allowed to participate in a non-classroom instructional experience. This is helpful for Sunday School and church leaders because if we want boys to learn the basic stories in the Bible, the theology, and the biblical principles, it may be better to do it in a non-classroom situation. (Take them out in the woods and/or do things that are active that involve the intended biblical content to be taught.) Now, where is that in the Bible? It's not.

Though Dr. Joy, as a Christian, did approach his study with a "regenerate" mind; he still found truth that was not written in God's word. We would not have become aware of his findings by just looking at the Bible, but it is very helpful research that complements the Bible.

Other Examples

Is "intermittent reinforcement" as effective as "continuous reinforcement"? B.F. Skinner conducted a study on this topic which produced helpful information.

What about Freud's "defense mechanisms"? Though those will be dealt with later, it can be stated here that there is much to be learned that can be helpful to the Christian when studying Freud's writings about defense mechanisms.

Other topics studied and written about are birth order and forms of discipline. There are a number of very informative books on those subjects that have been helpful to Christians in raising their children. Books regarding the family dynamics and the parenting dynamics that affect the development of children's personalities are all "nuggets" of information that are "out there" to be "reclaimed" by the believer and used to glorify God.

Research provided by Wilder Pennfield complements Biblical teaching of a soul/spirit. That will be discussed in Chapter 3. In other words, numerous ideas and discoveries have been made that are helpful "nuggets" that can't be found in Scripture.

THE COMMON GRACE OF GOD

Dr. David Plaster wrote that there are gifts that are bestowed upon non-Christians by the "common grace of God." He defines that common grace as: "The innumerable blessings, not a part of salvation that God, in His grace, gives to all people, even those that deserve death and will not be saved."[75] Or, said more simply, "God allows non-Christians to stumble upon truth." God allows those with unregenerate minds to discover truth in His universe.

So how do we know this to be true -- that God allows non-Christians to discover truth? First of all, we see it to be true. But why don't we take a look at some of the scriptural support for this assertion. Does the Scripture indicate that non-Christians can find truth in the world?

SCRIPTURAL INDICATIONS OF GOD'S BESTOWAL OF TRUTH TO NON-CHRISTIANS

Proverbs 22:2 says, "Rich and poor have this in common: The Lord is the Maker of them all." Look also at Proverbs 29:13 and Matthew 5:45.

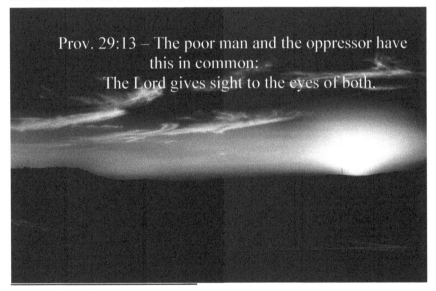

Prov. 29:13 – The poor man and the oppressor have this in common: The Lord gives sight to the eyes of both.

---

[75] Dave Plaster, Power Point slide from Class Lecture "Systematic Theology," Grace Theological Seminary, 2003.

Matthew 5:45 – ". . . He causes his sun to rise on the evil and the good, and sends rain on the righteous and the unrighteous."

And if we broaden those ideas beyond sight[76] and rain, is it probable that God lets some unrighteous people be smart and allows some righteous people to be "not-so-smart." It has nothing to do with who is going to heaven or who isn't. He just allows brilliance to come to a variety of different people.

Of course, the best brilliance can only come when you know God -- if you are talking about the kind of brilliance that also includes wisdom. And certainly biblical wisdom can only come from knowing God. The Bible states that the wise man says, "There is a God," while the fool says that there isn't (Ps. 14:1). So we know that biblical wisdom, certainly, comes only from following God and understanding what He has to say. But the non-Christian can also be brilliant and produce amazing contributions for our world.

The next scriptural passage provides several issues to consider. 1 Corinthians 15:33 says, "Do not be misled: 'Bad company corrupts good character.'" If you hang around bad people, sometimes you end up doing bad things. And notice that it is a quote. Paul is quoting someone when he spoke those words of warning.

The very compelling fact to consider, as it relates to our discussion of whether non-Christians can contribute to the Christian's world, is that this quotation is from a Greek comedy. "The Greek comedy, 'Thais,' was written by the Greek poet/philosopher, Menander,[77] whose writings, the Corinthians

---

[76] *Wallpapers* by Eric Shafer, "Tuscan Sunset" By alx2056 January 1st, 2010   Free High-Resolution Wallpapers
http://interfacelift.com/wallpaper_beta/email/2124/tuscan_sunset.html (Permission obtained for use.)

[77] Picture of Menander from
http://en.wikipedia.org/wiki/File:Menander_Chiaramonti_Inv1453.jpg. I, the copyright holder of this work, release this work into the public domain. This applies worldwide. In some countries this may not be legally possible; if so: *I grant anyone the right to use this work **for any purpose**, without any conditions, unless such conditions are required by law.*

would know."[78] Paul used a principle that was propagated by a Greek comedy and from a Greek poet/philosopher, and said, "This is true." In fact, the accepted principle that was observed and proclaimed by Menander, became biblical. It is now part of Scripture!

Could Paul have used ideas from Freud, or Skinner, or Rogers? He could have, if those psychologists found truth in the world. Bad company DOES corrupt good character. Paul knew that to be true and used the information to make his point, to teach the Corinthians and us, and in the end, to glorify God.

What about the statement in Titus 1:12, 13 which says, "Even one of their own prophets has said, 'Cretans are always liars, evil brutes, lazy gluttons,' This testimony is true"? Paul is again quoting someone. He says it is "true." Who is he quoting? Paul is quoting Epimenides[79] (a sixth-century B.C. native of Knossos, Crete), who was held in high esteem by the Cretans."[80] He, Epimenides, said that the Cretans were "always liars, evil brutes, and lazy gluttons." (He was definitely not politically correct by today's standards!) Paul  says, "He's right!" Paul is using a secular figure and pointing out the validity of Epimenides's "findings," his "observations." So, when one considers the above evidences, it seems clear that even in Scripture there is an acceptance of the fact that truth can be learned from unbelievers.

Those with regenerate minds do not always have whole truth, however. Though certainly with regenerate minds we have the capability of understanding God, we are not always correct in all of our thinking. We

---

[78] Kenneth Barker, Gen. Ed., *The NIV Study Bible* (Grand Rapids: Zondervan Bible Publishers, 1985), 1757 -- Footnote for 1 Corinthians 15:33.

[79] Picture of Epimenides from http://commons.wikimedia.org/wiki/File:Homeros_MFA_Munich_272.jpg. I, the copyright holder of this work, release this work into the public domain. This applies worldwide. In some countries this may not be legally possible; if so: *I grant anyone the right to use this work **for any purpose**, without any conditions, unless such conditions are required by law.*

[80] Kenneth Barker, Gen. Ed., *The NIV Study Bible*, (Grand Rapids: Zondervan Bible Publishers, 1985) 1851 -- Footnote for Titus 1:12.

continue to grow and learn throughout life.

So the idea that "if you have a regenerate mind, then you can know truth, but people with unregenerate minds cannot discover any truth" is not supported by Scripture. In reality, some Christian people have some "wacky" ideas and some non-Christian people have ideas that make a lot of sense.

Now, with regenerate minds we can go further in finding truth because we can have wisdom. We can know God and know what He is trying to tell us. And so, certainly, there is truth there, but be careful of embracing an extreme position that says that if you have a regenerate mind, it must mean you have a nearly perfect mind.

And conversely, avoid espousing the belief that having an unregenerate mind means that the non-Christian has nothing of any worth to contribute. An unregenerate person can stumble upon truth and be accurate in many of his perceptions. He can produce much that can be of value to the Christian. Discernment is the key to knowing what to accept when one considers what the non-Christian has to offer.

DISCERNMENT

Before concluding this chapter, the idea of "discernment" needs to be addressed. Hebrews 5:14 says, "But solid food is for those who are mature and who by constant use have *trained* themselves to *distinguish good from evil.*"

Our job as Christians is to study the Bible and then to study secular psychology -- making the distinction between good and evil. Ask yourself, "Am I able to filter out the bad?" Can you make your "grid" tight enough? To have a tight grid means that you have to have a strong understanding of the Word of God so that when you study materials other than the Bible, you can bring those materials through your grid and allow only the good and truthful things to come through. Hopefully, as you bring theories through, you can weed out the things that are contradictory to Scripture and keep the things that are complementary.

Philippians 1:9-10 says, "And this is my prayer: that your love may abound more and more in knowledge and depth of insight, so you may be *able to discern what is best* and may be pure and blameless until the day of Christ."

That is the real key to the question of integration -- the discernment of good from evil. We want to accept what is true, but we need to have a *practiced* "truth-finder," so that we can be discerning and accurate as we make the distinctions between good and evil. We want to be able to differentiate between what to keep and what to discard. The more mature the believer and the more practiced he is in knowing God's word and applying it to his world, the easier it will be to make those determinations and the clearer it will be as to what to keep and what to discard.

Conclusion – Is the Bible Sufficient?

So, what is the grand conclusion of this? How do we address the question: "Is the Bible sufficient?" Do we who dabble in psychology assume that the Bible is not sufficient? If we are Christians, obviously not!

Of course the Bible is sufficient. 2 Peter 1:3 says, "His divine power has given us everything we need for life and godliness through our knowledge of Him." God's divine power has given us *everything* we need to know for life, through His word. And godliness comes through our knowledge of Him.

So here is the answer: Sufficient? Absolutely! The Bible answers all foundational and important questions about life. It tells how to find God, know God, and serve God. It is sufficient.

But is it exhaustive? (That is what many Christians are really wanting to know when they ask if the Bible is sufficient.) Does it tell us everything we could possibly know in the realm of psychology? No! The Bible is *not* exhaustive on any topic -- including psychology. It wasn't intended to be. So where it is not exhaustive, it is important that we study the subject -- being careful what we bring through our biblical "grid."

Some believe that we should only read the Bible. But the Bible itself says, "Subdue your world," "Have dominion over your world" (Gen. 1:28). We need to understand it well in order to subdue and rule over it well.

When it comes to the medical community, most Christians agree whole-heartedly that it is important to study and understand. But it is true in every other facet of life, including psychology.

So build a solid biblical foundation and then go out and study the world. Be open to what God will demonstrate of Himself through that study.

CHAPTER 3
PERSONALITY: PART 1

Now we turn to the topic of personality. What does it mean to have personality? Does God have a personality? How does our soul/spirit affect our personality? Is it possible to have more than one personality? What does the Bible say about the subject of personality?

This chapter will delve into topics that may seem strange at times, but are necessary to explore in order to fully understand the idea of personhood and personality. As you read through this chapter, allow yourself to assess the ideas presented (even though they may initially seem irrelevant or unusual) and consider how each topic impacts the idea of personality.

"Faces"

Our personality consists of a "persona" that we portray to others -- our "face."[81] Our "persona" is our outward appearance. This is what we show people. Webster's dictionary states that persona is "an individual's social façade or front -- that especially in the analytic psychology of C. G.

---

[81] Image purchased from dreamstime.com. Royalty-free image up to 500,000 copies. © Lesya Castillo | Dreamstime.com. Title: "Theater Masks."

Jung reflects the role in life the individual is playing."[82]

The Hebrew word for face, "panim," is plural.[83] What is God trying to tell us? Why isn't it singular? Could it be that God is suggesting that we wear many "faces" as part of our "persona"? Why would that be or not be legitimate? Does that mean we have different personalities?

The Diagnostic and Statistical Manual for psychological disorders (DMS-IV-TR) formerly had a diagnosis called "Multiple Personality Disorder." Consider that diagnosis for a minute. Would that be a valid diagnosis for the Christian? Can you have more than one personality or do you just have one personality that comes out in different forms? Those are all good questions.

The Bible teaches that we do wear "faces" in the sense that we have different aspects to our personality and they don't always match up with our "heart." We demonstrate those aspects through different emotions or sometimes through pretense. Those different "faces" that we show can come out in legitimate ways and sometimes in illegitimate ways.

We may don an illegitimate "face" when we are trying to portray ourselves as being something that we're not. Why would a person do that? We often do that so that others will think better of us and/or because we are hiding something. When we attempt to hide who we are, we are invoking a "Self-Enhancing" and "Self-Protective" strategy (which will be discussed in chapter 4).

What faces might we wear? Did you put on a "happy" face today? Why do we put on our "happy face"? Maybe we don't want anyone to feel sorry for us. Maybe we want others to think we are "all together." Maybe we want others to like us, to be drawn to us, or to respect us. Maybe we want attention.

Or my "happy face" could be legitimately portraying the feeling of well-being that just exudes from me. Sometimes a happy face is just that -- a happy face that is showing what is truly deep down.

What other faces do we have? In the movie, *Shrek*, the donkey is asked, "Why the long face?" Of course, that was his normal face! But

[82]Merriam-Webster, *Webster's Ninth New Collegiate Dictionary* (Springfield, MA: Merriam-Webster Inc., Publishers, 1983), p. 877.

[83] Francis Brown, S. R. Driver & Charles A. Briggs, *A Hebrew and English Lexicon of the Old Testament* (Oxford: Clarendon Press, 1978), p. 815.

what would a "long face" portray for us? Why would we choose to put on a "long face" or a sad face? Do some people wear the sad face all the time? What could a sad face accomplish for us?

Maybe it could be a way of getting attention. The sad, "long" face may influence some people to pity the wearer. Could it also help me to shirk from facing reality?

And yet, sadness could be my real face! So we need to be aware that when we look at someone's face, his persona, her outward appearance, it could be real! It could be indicating exactly what's going on. And yet, it could also be self-protective and self-enhancing.

THE EXAMPLE OF SAMUEL AND DAVID

WITH ELIAB

In 1 Samuel 16:1-7, the Bible gives an example of how the outward "face" and the heart can look different. In this passage, the story is told of Samuel, who takes a trip to the house of Jesse to anoint a king. In the process, Samuel evaluates the persona of each son who comes before him.

Look at what it says: ". . . 'Fill your horn with oil and be on your way; I am sending you to Jesse of Bethlehem. I have chosen one of his sons to be king' . . . Samuel did what the Lord said. When he arrived at Bethlehem, the elders of the town trembled when they met him. They asked, 'Do you come in peace?' Samuel replied, 'Yes, in peace; I have come to sacrifice to the Lord. Consecrate yourselves and come to the sacrifice with me.' Then he consecrated Jesse and his sons and invited them to the sacrifice. When they arrived, Samuel saw Eliab and thought, 'Surely the Lord's anointed stands here before the Lord.' But the Lord said to Samuel, 'Do not consider his appearance or his height, for I have rejected him. The Lord does not look at the things man looks at. Man looks at the outward appearance, but the Lord looks at the heart.'"

"Man looks at the *outward appearance*, but the Lord looks at the *heart*." God is trying to tell us that there are two aspects here. There is the "persona" -- what is portrayed outwardly and can be observed by others -- and there is what is really inside. God is talking about the "faces" that people wear. Sometimes that can match up with what is inside and sometimes it doesn't. The Lord looks at the heart.

The first son to be observed by Samuel was Eliab. Eliab must have been a handsome young man -- tall, muscular, athletic-looking. Maybe as the oldest son he had an air of leadership-like confidence. The Bible says that Samuel's response to seeing Eliab was, "Surely the Lord's anointed stands here before the Lord." Samuel must have been thinking, "Okay, there he is. I mean, you talk about King material, here's the guy!" But God said, "Don't look at that"

Sometimes we think the very same things! We think, "But, I talked to him! He has a good personality. He's very confident. He has a commanding presence. He's a good leader."

But God said to Samuel, "I've rejected him. I've got somebody else in mind."

And David wasn't even there! They had to go "round him up." He was "ruddy." He had a handsome, yet kind of rough appearance, and evidently, was not the kind of person who would give the initial impression as being "king material!"

But what was it about Eliab that was so bad? Why didn't God choose him? What was wrong with his heart? Take a look at the next chapter.

Chapter 17, verse 28 says, "When Eliab, David's oldest brother, heard him speaking with the men, he burned with anger at him and asked, 'Why have you come down here? And with whom did you leave those few sheep in the desert? I know how conceited you are and how wicked your heart is; you came down only to watch the battle."

Little brother, David, came to the battle to bring food to his brothers and to see how they were doing because Dad told him to. You'd think that older brother would say, "Hey! Thanks for coming and for bringing the food. You know, we are kind of hungry."

But Eliab said in essence, "You insolent brat!! I know why you're here. You conceited, arrogant, little fool you! You just wanted to see the battle!"

David must have been thinking, "What did I do? I just came to check on you and to bring food!"

What happed with Eliab? There was something sinful going on in his heart.

The Bible says, "He BURNED with anger. It seems evident in that passage that "Somebody's got an issue here! He's got some real 'psychological' problems!" Eliab's anger was hot beyond what it should have been. There was something sinful going on inside.

Emotions are signals as to what is happening inside. Sometimes passionate anger is appropriate. But if we are "hot" beyond what we ought to be, that is when it is time to take a look inside and ask why. When emotions come out with that intensity, it's a good signal to look and see what is motivating the reaction. It is a good time to look at the heart.

What is going on with Eliab that he snaps at David like that? "You insolent brat! I know why you're here. You're here to see the battle. You conceited, little kid you! Who'd you leave those few sheep with, in the desert?"

Whoa! What is going on? He's lying. He's being demeaning. He's accusing. He's belittling David's job as sheepherder. He's accusing him of being irresponsible.

Why do older brothers sometimes do that? Is that an indication of jealousy? What would Eliab have been jealous of David about? Eliab is tall. David is average. Eliab is handsome. Why would he be jealous of his younger brother?

Could it be that Eliab remembered David being anointed as king? Could it be that as he was introduced to Samuel, he thought, "I've got this one 'in the bag,' This is mine," only to learn that Samuel did not pick him.

And when Samuel directed that David be brought in from tending the sheep, David was anointed IN FRONT of all of his brothers! Can you imagine what was going through Eliab's mind? It doesn't appear that Eliab was thinking of congratulating David and honoring him for his future status as king.

In fact, when Eliab did get a chance to express his feelings to David, he said, "I know how conceited your heart is!" (Isn't it amazing how many times the jealous one accuses the other of the very jealousy and conceit that he has in his own heart.)[84] Eliab was telling David, "I know how arrogant you are!" What was Eliab doing?

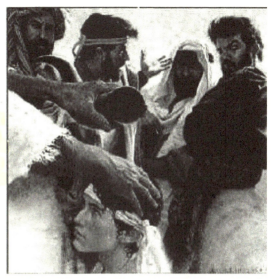

Freud came up with a term to describe what was occurring with Eliab. He called it "projection." Eliab was projecting his "stuff" onto his little brother. So, instead of being happy for David, he accused David of the very things that he was feeling. He accused David of being wicked in his heart -- needy for self-importance and inclusion (by wanting to see the battle). He accused David of being proud, arrogant, and dishonest. Though Eliab was being "insolent," he accused David of being that way.

Maybe that was part of Eliab's "heart" and maybe that was what God saw when he rejected Eliab. Maybe God was thinking, "I don't want somebody who's arrogant, somebody who's conceited, somebody who thinks he is so great! I want to pick somebody who is a man after My heart." David was called "a man after God's heart" (1 Samuel 13:14; Acts 13:22) several times in Scripture. Even when David "messed up" in tremendous ways, he was still a man after God's heart.

So sometimes we look at people and think, "Wow! That's who I would pick." We may think, "They are close to God. They know how to 'do' life!" And sometimes we get fooled. Even the prophet, Samuel, was fooled; so we also can be fooled.

---

[84] Picture from clipart.christiansunite.com. "You may download images for personal or commercial use, or for use on web sites." Accessed 1.24.11.

BEING A "REAL" CHRISTIAN

"Faces" can even be a part of our present Christian world -- in Christian circles, at church, at youth group meetings, on a Christian college campus, etc. One face that we like to wear is the *"spiritual" face*. If we are at a secular university or at a ball game or at our job in the secular world, it's probably not as important to wear a "spiritual" face; but if one is reading this textbook as part of a psychology class in a Christian setting, the reader may feel the pressure to wear the "spiritual face."

Pharisee and the Publican by James Tissot

In what ways could we portray a "spiritual" face? The Bible talks about this when it refers to the Pharisees who made long and lengthy prayers and who "love to pray standing in the synagogues and on the street corners to be seen by men"[85] (Matt. 6:5,7). In our present day, what ways might we fake spirituality using self-seeking goals?

We could get heavily involved in a chapel ministry, missions group, Bible study, or prayer ministry as a demonstration of our "spirituality" without true conviction. We could simulate deep emotional concern or praise, maybe using prayer requests as a way of advertising ourselves -- our "good works" and "godly activities or interest." We could flaunt our memory of Scripture passages or use the "spiritual" language and words that are not a normal part of our vocabulary. We could lead a chapel service or a Bible study in order to be seen, admired, and commended while hoping to be "popular" or "famous." Or we could advertise our "spirituality" by portraying any of the above

---

[85]Picture of Pharisee praying from Pharisee and the Publican James Tissot (1836-1902/French) © *SuperStock* Usage: Jan, 27, 2011, Industry: Education, For Use in Biblical Psychology Textbook, License fee: $0.00.
http://www.superstock.com/stock-photos-images/999-178

through photographs or writings that are found in prominent places or through some other type of conspicuous media.

Whether we are tempted to put on a "spiritual face" or not, we are also confronted with another phenomenon in Christian circles. We come in contact with others who wear "spiritual faces" and we can be "drawn in" to accepting the falsehood of their spiritual facade.

However, we want to be careful *not* to look at everyone who appears to be "spiritual" and deeply convicted about his or her relationship with God, and assume that person is just "wearing a face." Probably a good percentage of the people we come in contact with are sincere in their portrayal of their beliefs and convicted in their hearts. We don't want to become cynical and assume that those who appear to be close to God are just "faking it." But a common assumption of young Christians is that all who claim to be Christ-followers and appear to have a deep, convicting faith are what they portray themselves to be. In reality, however, that's not true. Illegitimate faces are not *only* worn by those who function in the secular world, they are worn by those in the "religious world" and even sometimes by true Christians. The better reaction would be to find some guidelines for ascertaining if the faces we are seeing are real.

Ask yourself, "Is that the real person?" It could be. Maybe the demonstration of godliness is real. Maybe he or she is very close to God and deeply touched by his or her relationship with Him. But it could also be that he or she is demonstrating a self-enhancing, self-protective strategy.[86]

God gives us some ideas on how to know who His true followers are and who are the ones that aren't really as committed to Him as they appear. John 13:35 says, "By this all men will know that you are my disciples, if you love one another." Love can be a key indicator. We can get hints of what is inside when we observe the type of love that is shown to others -- especially those of a lower rank, whom we assess as somehow inferior to us in some way, or those who are close to us -- like family members. But sometimes people can deceive us there too.

Christ also pointed out examples that were portrayed by the Pharisees. He said in Matthew 23, that their outer "face" was "whitewashed," but the

---

[86]"Strategies" are discussed in my book entitled: *Theological Foundations of Counseling*, Thomas J. Edgington, Ph. D., Edgington Publicatons. Printed by Lulu, 2014.

inner self was as a "tomb" -- "full of dead men's bones and everything unclean" (v. 27). He said that their "cup and dish" were clean on the outside, but inside "full of greed and self-indulgence" (v. 25). When we look at Matthew 23, we find that one measurement of the "inner self" is if the "spiritual" person shows "justice, mercy, and faithfulness" (v. 23). How do they treat others (especially those "under" them) in day-to-day relationships? That is a key.

And humility is an important indicator. How much do they talk about themselves, publicizing their works and commending their behaviors before men? The "spiritual-looking" can be very cunning in the ways they find to advertise their "good deeds." Matthew 23 highlights this problem, citing their love of the "places of honor at banquets," for people to acknowledge their "elevated" title of Rabbi when they are greeted, and their prayers that advertise their "goodness" to others. And there are more examples of their self-exaltation. Compare that to the humility shown by the tax collector in Luke 18:10-14 whose prayer disclosed his sinfulness.

How much time do they devote to joyfully and sincerely lessening the burdens of others? Matthew 23:4 tells us how the illegitimately "spiritual" "tie up heavy loads and put them on men's shoulders; but they themselves are not willing to lift a finger to move them."

Be on your guard against the "yeast" of the modern day Pharisees and Sadducees (Matt. 16:5). Samuel was fooled and we can be too. So be aware that falsehood occurs, even in "religious" settings.

This section is not intended to cause you to doubt the sincerity of others, only to challenge you to look at yourself and others and ask yourself, "What faces do I wear and what ones do I see others wearing?" The purpose of the questions is to promote thinking and the taking of some time to look at the unique strategies that take place -- even in the Christian "culture." There are people who are part of the "religious" world who have their own cunning ways of getting their needs met apart from God while appearing to be close to God. Ask yourself, "Is this the real face and the real style of relating? Or could this be a portrayal of an image that is not real?"

Carl Rogers talked about being *congruent*. "Congruence is when the outward demonstration of self, accurately matches what is being felt on the inside. It constitutes the 'state' of a person who is 'genuine', 'whole', 'integrated', 'without facade', 'adjusted.'" [87] Incongruence is shown when the inside and the outside do not match up. It involves defensiveness, denial (or distortion), falseness or deceit.[88] Sometimes it is conscious and sometimes it is not.

So what does it mean to be an authentic, genuine person? What does it mean for me to live out who I really am? For the Christian, what does it mean to be a REAL Christian? That's a great question because it may mean that I don't always present myself as having it all together. Maybe it means that sometimes I let you know where I sin and where I mess up.

There is a danger to do that with some people or groups because there are those that will say, "Oh really? I don't think we want you anymore -- especially as a leader, or pastor, or teacher. We want somebody who has it together."

Though it may not be appropriate to air out "dirty laundry" with everyone, it is helpful to have a trusted source to divulge the reality of our sinful struggles. (Total nakedness is not always appropriate in a sinful world, but more apt to be appropriate in a trusted relationship.)

Do any of us have it "all together?" Even those who look like they have it "all together," don't. Even those who are clean, neat, and smiling, DON'T have it all together. And if you spent an extended period of time

---

[87]C. R. Rogers, "A Theory of Therapy, Personality and Interpersonal Relationships, as Developed in the Client-Centered Framework," in S. Koch (Ed.), *A Study of a Science: Vol. 3. Formulations of the Person and the Social Context* (New York: McGraw-Hill, 1959), 206.

And, C. R. Rogers, "The Necessary and Sufficient Conditions for Therapeutic Personality Change," *Journal of Consulting Psychology* (1957)," in H. Kirschenbaum & V. L. Henderson (Eds.), *The Carl Rogers Reader* (Houghton Mifflin Company: Boston, 1989), 224.

This is all quoted in a paper posted on the Internet by Ivan Ellingham. His article is entitled, "Carl Rogers' 'Congruence' as an Organismic Not a Freudian Concept" (in Wyatt, G. (ed) *Congruence: Rogers' Therapeutic Conditions* published by PCCS Books, 2001) http://www.allanturner.co.uk/papers/congruence_iv.htm accessed on 2/17/09 -- Section "In the Footsteps of Sigmund."

[88]C. R. Rogers, *On Becoming a Person: A Therapist's View of Psychotherapy* (Boston: Houghton Mifflin, 1961), 341.

with anyone, you would learn that person was not all that he or she appeared to be. So what does it mean for you to be a REAL Christian? What does it mean for your outward face to be a congruent portrayal of what is inside?

Though imperfect, David was a REAL God-follower. Christ was real yet, of course, He didn't have sin. So what does it mean to have a sin nature and to be real, and yet be a man or woman after God's heart? That's an important question.

Sometimes a relationship can continue for years before the true "face" immerges. Sometimes we can be deceived. But the true face is always a reflection of the heart. And the Bible has something to say about that. It talks about the heart. The "heart" is the word that the Bible uses to denote the "real" inward person -- wearing no mask or illegitimate "face."

Personality has more to do with the heart -- the real person. Persona is the outward expression of the heart (even though it can be deceptive).

Personhood

WHAT IS A PERSON?

So what is personality? If we begin by removing the last three letters (i-t-y) of the word, we have the word "personal." What does "personal" mean? The suffix "al" simply means: of, relating to, or characterized by."[89] If something is "personal," it is "of, relating to, or characterized by" a person. According to the *American Heritage Dictionary*, the next suffix: "ity," means: "the quality, state, or degree."[90] So, to put it all together, personality is: "the quality, state, or degree of, that which is of, relating to, or characterized by, a person."

The definition seems to focus on the aspects of a person. But if that is our definition and our definition is to be understood, then the next question should probably be, "What is a person?" "What is personhood?"

---

[89]*American Heritage Dictionary*, 2nd college edition (Boston: Houghton-Mifflin Co., 1985), 91.

[90]*American Heritage Dictionary*, p. 681.

In order to understand personality, we have to understand "personhood." What does it mean to be a person? What distinguishes us as persons? -- Free will? -- Consciousness?

Animals have a type of "consciousness." How are we different from them?

Look at some of what the dictionary says. A person is: "A living human being, esp. as distinguished from an animal or thing . . . the living body of a human being."[91] "A human being" . . . Do you agree with that? Next, it says, "A living body" -- as opposed to a dead one. You are a person if you don't have a dead body, but have a living body. Are there any problems with that definition? -- Human beings? -- A living body?

GOD, ANGELS, SATAN, AFTER DEATH
-- PERSONS?

If that explanation is accepted as the all-encompassing definition of what a person is, then **God** -- that is: Father, Son, and Holy Spirit (before Christ took on a body) -- is not considered a person. God is not a human being. The second person of the Trinity took on a body, but the Father and the Holy Spirit did not take on a body. John 4:24 makes it clear that God is a spirit. The incarnation occurred when the second person of the Trinity took on a human body, but before that He did not have a human body. Some believe that the Godhead is now housed in a body -- happening after Christ resurrected and went back to heaven (Acts 7:55, 56). (We will discuss this later under the heading, "Are Bodies Important to God?" pages 118-121.)

---

[91] *American Heritage Dictionary* (Boston: Houghton Mifflin Company, 1985), p. 925.

Are angels persons? According to the previous definition, **angels** would not be persons. But angels are personal! They emote. They choose. They think. They relate. They appear to be persons, though there are many people that don't believe that. Yet, angels[92] are called the "sons of God" (Job 1:6). If they are the "sons of God," could that mean that they are persons?

When Scripture talks about "the sons of," what does that mean? It means: "having the characteristics of." When we talk about angels, we talk about them having the "characteristics of God."

When Christ came to earth, He said, "I am the 'Son of God.' -- I have the characteristics of God." That's why the people wanted to stone Him (John 10:36). Christ was saying that He had the characteristics of God. When He referred to himself as the "Son of Man" (Mark 10:33, etc.) -- which was His favorite term -- what He was saying was, "I have the characteristics of a man." The people listening were probably thinking, "Yeah. That's obvious!" But Christ was trying to communicate, "You don't understand. I'm a man! This is a big deal for me! I HAVE always been God. Now I'm a man."

So when angels are called "Sons of God" (Job 1:6) -- meaning that they have the characteristics of God -- it appears that indicates they are persons. They are made in God's image and likeness. Even though the Bible does not say that directly, the reference to their being "sons of God" seems to allude to that fact.

Satan would not be a person under the dictionary definition. Some people want to think about evil as a "force" and Satan as a "force." No. Satan is a PERSON! According to the *American Heritage Dictionary*, that wouldn't fit.

---

[92] Angel picture from http://karenswhimsy.com/public-domain-images/free-christian-clipart/free-christian-clipart-4.htm. Public domain, free Christian Clipart. Accessed 1/19/11.

And **after death** we would not be persons because we would no longer be connected to a living body. Our bodies would be dead. So, according to the dictionary, we would not be considered persons anymore. The Bible doesn't say that. It assumes that after death, we are still persons (Revelation 6:9, Hebrews 12:23).

CONCLUSION AND DEFINITION OF PERSON

The point that is being made here is that many times when we think of persons, we think of us. We think of persons as human beings. We start at the wrong place.

The goal here is to rearrange our thinking, to start with God. God is a person. That is our starting point -- our presupposition. And God made us like Himself. He made us persons. So a person is anyone who is "like God." That is our definition.

DOES A PERSON NEED A BODY?

The next topic is one that we don't often consider. Is a body necessary to be a person? Given the previous definition of person -- "Anyone who is 'like God,'" what do you think? Does a person need a body?

According to our chosen definition based on biblical principles, *American Heritage Dictionary* is wrong. A person is NOT a living body. A person is anyone like God; therefore, you can be a person without a body. God the Father, God the Holy Spirit, and, God the son (before the incarnation when He took on a body) are/were all persons. That is what we call the *"persons"* of the Trinity.

A body is not necessary to be a person. "God is a spirit and they that worship Him, worship Him in spirit and in truth" (John 4:24). God is a spirit being. There is some entity there. He's not a blob. There is an entity called "spirit."

God is a spirit; therefore, God must have created us as spiritual beings. That's part of being in the image and likeness of God.

So it is not necessary to have a body to be a person; however, a body

IS necessary to be a complete human being. To be everything that God intended us to be as human beings, He gave us bodies. He could have made us spirits alone, but He didn't. God gave us bodies and those bodies are necessary to complete our humanity.

In fact, without the body we are said to be "naked." Second Corinthians 5:2, 3 says we "groan." "Meanwhile we groan, longing to be clothed with our heavenly dwelling, because when we are clothed, we will not be found naked." We long for the body.

The next verse (verse 4) states, "For while we are in this tent, we groan and are burdened, because we do not wish to be unclothed but to be clothed with our heavenly dwelling. . . ." We want to be reunited.

So when we die, we no longer have bodies. The body is dead. It gets buried. We (our spirits) go to heaven or hell. But we long to be reunited with our bodies. We want to get back with our bodies again, and God is going to do that. He is going to bring our bodies back.

Why is this important? You might be thinking, "Why are we talking about bodies? Why is it important to know whether spirits have bodies to understand personhood? Why is that a big deal?" Because maybe how we look at people's bodies and their spirits blended together, affects how we relate to others and how we view ourselves. And that affects our view of psychology

DOES DEATH DESTROY PERSONHOOD?

Does death destroy personhood? Death simply means "separation." This is a very important point.

The spirit does not die, but it does leave the body. In Luke 23:46, Christ said, "Father, into your hands, I commit my spirit." In James 2:26, the passage is talking about faith and works, but in that context it says, "The body without the spirit is dead." From those two passages, you get the idea that death is not the cessation of your heart or your brain. Death means the spirit left the body. [93]   And this author believes that death occurs when the spirit leaves the brain.

THE EXPERIMENTS OF WILDER PENFIELD

If we were to decide in what organ of the body the spirit resides, it would probably be the brain. Though that cannot be proven, fascinating research by Wilder Penfield[94] shed some light on the subject and also introduced other interesting points.

In the 1900s Wilder Penfield, a surgeon for epileptic patients, made some amazing discoveries. After removing part of the skull to expose the brain of his patient and with the person being awake and conscious, Penfield maneuvered an electrode to pinpoint the area in the brain responsible for his/her seizures.[95] In the process, Penfield also found that when stimulating different areas of the brain, he obtained different responses.[96] "The tip of his electrode elicited in his patients, dreams, smells, long-lost memories, auditory and visual hallucinations and even out-of-body

---

[93] Picture of spirit leaving body from Photobucket.com, by sonicnova11, http://media.photobucket.com/image/spiritual%20body/sonicnova11/astral-projection.jpg?o=31. By displaying or publishing ("posting") any Content on or through the Photobucket Services, you hereby grant to Photobucket and other users a non-exclusive, fully paid and royalty-free, worldwide, limited license to use, modify, delete from, add to, publicly perform, publicly display, reproduce and translate such Content, including without limitation distributing part or all of the Site in any media formats through any media channels, except Content marked "private" will not be distributed outside the Photobucket Services. Photobucket and/or other Users may copy, print or display publicly available Content outside of the Photobucket Services, including without limitation, via the Site or third party websites or applications.

[94] Image of Wilder Penfield By YUL89YYZ at en.wikipedia [Public domain]

[95] Wilder Penfield, *The Mystery of the Mind*, (Princeton, NJ: Princeton University Press, 1975), pp. 12,13.

[96] Penfield pp. 21-27.

experiences."[97]

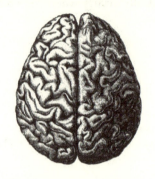

Penfield kept track of the particular areas that elicited a specific response by placing a small square piece of paper, numbered or lettered, on the precise point on the brain's surface where the response occurred.[98]   He noted that when returning to that place and simulating it again, he consistently obtained the same response from that area.   He recorded what "thoughts, behaviours and sensations arose from the excitation of specific parts of the cortex."[99]

Penfield wrote:

On the first occasion, when one of these "flashbacks'" was reported to me by a conscious patient (1933), I was incredulous. On each subsequent occasion, I marveled. For example, when a mother told me she was suddenly aware, as my electrode touched the cortex, of being in her kitchen listening to the voice of her little boy who was playing outside in the yard. She was aware of the neighborhood noises, such as passing motor cars, that might mean danger to him. A young man stated he was sitting at a baseball game in a small town and watching a little boy crawl under the fence to join the audience. Another was in a concert hall listening to music. "An orchestration," he explained. He

---

[97]Picture of brain from http://commons.wikimedia.org/wiki/File:Human_brain.png Size of this preview: 569 × 600 pixels (577 × 608 pixels, file size: 290 KB, MIME type: image/png) Medical diagram of human brain. *This image (or other media file) is in the public domain because its copyright has **expired***.

[98]Mo Constandi, "Wilder Penfield, Neural Cartographer" Category: History of Neuroscience • *Medicine & Health* (Information cited, found 3 paragraphs above actual exposed brain picture), http://scienceblogs.com/neurophilosophy/2008/08/wilder_penfield_neural_cartographer. php   Posted on: August 27, 2008 5:30 P,M Copyright ©2005-2009 ScienceBlogs LLC (Accessed 2/13/09).

[99]Vaughn, "Charting the Brain's Unknown Territory," Posted on August 28, 2008 02:00 PM, http://www.mindhacks.com/blog/2008/08/wilder_penfield_ch.html (1 February 2009).

could hear the different instruments. All these were important events, but recalled with complete detail. D. F. [another patient] could hear instruments playing a melody. I restimulated the same point thirty times (!) trying to mislead her, and dictated each response to a stenographer. Each time I re-stimulated, she heard the melody again.[100] I warned her I was going to stimulate, but I did not do so. "Nothing."[101]

What an amazing discovery! Memories and senses can be triggered by touching different places in the brain!

Yet Penfield was baffled as he observed this phenomenon and began to wrestle with one issue. "There was always a restless wondering within me about the working of the brain and its relation to mind. . . . Is the mind merely a function of the brain? Or is it a separate but closely related element?[102] . . . Which is the more reasonable . . . that man's being is based on one element, (physical -- brain) or on two (physical and spiritual -- brain + mind)?" [103]

In simpler terms, one could express it like this: There are neuro-mechanisms in the brain that can explain memory. But there is also a person who is talking about the memory! There seem to be two entities. The one is the "person." The other is the "brain." When using theanalogy of the computer and the programmer -- with the brain being the computer, [104] Penfield was saying that it was just like when you press certain keys on your computer in order to hear music. You still have to have somebody hitting the key or clicking the mouse to play the music.

---

[100] Penfield, pp. 21,22

[101] Penfield, p. 27.

[102] Penfield, p. x.

[103] Penfield, p. xiii.

[104] Picture Title: "Computer and Hand on Beach," © Nikolais, purchased from dreamstime.com.

You need to have someone aware of the possibilities and making the decision. The music is available to be played, but it doesn't just play on its own. It needs a programmer. It needs a "person" to press the key. "This suggests that the mind must have a supply of energy available to it for independent action. . . The mind directs and the mind-mechanism (the brain) executes."[105]

The mind must take data, make decisions, and interpret data. Yet, there is no "engram"[106] or physical space where that action can be observed or accounted for. There is no "'structural impression that psychical experience leaves on protoplasm.'"[107]

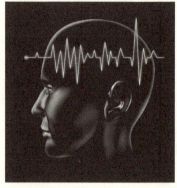

Penfield concluded, "For myself, after a professional lifetime spent in trying to discover how the brain accounts for the mind, it comes as a surprise now to discover, during this final examination of evidence, that the dualist hypothesis seems the more reasonable of the two possible explanations. . . . What a thrill it is, to discover that the scientist, too, can legitimately believe in the existence of the spirit!"[108]

Penfield even wondered (now remember, he is writing as a scientist and not a theologian), if minds go on after death and immortality may be a possibility![109] This comes from a scientist who was dabbling with brains! And he was seeing this. That's pretty amazing!

It is this author's contention, that the "mind" (both as we normally use the word and the way it is used in the Scripture) is another term for "spirit." When evaluating theologically the existence of the "mind" (or "spirit"), it is not simply a manifestation of the brain. The brain could possibly "house" the spirit, but they are still two separate entities that act independently of each other. The body (brain) and the spirit (mind) are

---

[105] Penfield, p. 46.

[106] Picture Title: "Brain stroke circulation heart pulse rate," purchased from dreamstime.com © Skypixel.

[107] Penfield, p. 6.

[108] Penfield, p. 85.

[109] Penfield, p. 87.

separate entities -- yet they are connected in such a way that it is impossible to separate them here on earth. They are intertwined like a tapestry, and only death can separate them. (That is why we must remain holistic in our thinking.) Penfield is giving scientific evidence that substantiates our theology.

So the relevance of Penfield's studies to our discussion is this: We are spiritual beings who are housed in a body. In this life we have two entities that are in relationship with each other -- body and spirit. But when the body dies, the spirit leaves the body. Yet the "person" continues to exist. The "person" is the spirit that endures.

OTHER THOUGHTS ABOUT THE SPIRIT'S LOCATION AND ASPECTS

Another proof of the location of your spirit being in your brain is as it relates to missing parts of the body. If you cut a leg off, the person is still there. If you remove the stomach, the person is still there. But if you take the brain, the person is gone. Being "brain-dead" carries with it the assumption that the spirit has left.

ARE BODIES IMPORTANT TO GOD?

So, if we are spiritual beings, are our bodies important to God? Take some time to think about that question. Are bodies important to God?

"Your body is a temple of the Holy Spirit . . ." (1 Corinthians 6:19). God created our bodies. We are not spirits alone.

It is important to note that God now has a body. In Acts 7:55, 56, Stephen described seeing the "Son of Man" (Jesus Christ) standing "at the right hand of God." In essence, Stephen was saying, "In the prominent place, I saw a man -- God in a body." That's HUGE! God now has a body -- Father, Son, Holy Spirit, in a body!

Christ had a new body, yet Mary didn't recognize Him at first when she saw Him in the garden. He had a new "adapted" body, yet a body. He had a resurrected, REAL body. We will have resurrected, REAL bodies, yet they will be perfected (whatever that means).

All of us will have perfect bodies. We will get the same bodies -- perfected. Our new body will be adapted for heavenly purposes. Yet Christ's body will have scars -- as a reminder.

What is God going to do with our earthly bodies? Romans 8:23 says that He will "redeem" them. God is going to put our bodies back together with our spirits. So it seems that bodies are important to God.

1 Corinthians 15:42-44 talks about the resurrection and the magnificence of our new bodies. It says, "So it will be with the resurrection of the dead. The body that is sown is perishable, it is raised imperishable; it is sown in dishonor, it is raised in glory; it is sown in weakness, it is raised in power; it is sown a natural body, it is raised a spiritual body. If there is a natural body, there is also a spiritual body." The word "it" (in this NIV translation) is used for both the "soulish" earthly body and the "spiritual" body that is raised in glory. The "it" that recurs in this translation, refers to the same essence though it is shown to have different functions. The "soul/soulish" body will be raised a "spiritual" body in glory.

But, how is God going to put my decayed body back together? Some bodies have been in graves for thousands of years. Think about the enormity of the resurrection -- bodies that have been dead for thousands of years will be reconstructed and made alive!

There is a historical story that has to do with that subject and the apples that grew from a tree planted over a grave. The somewhat comical, yet realistic question that is asked is, "Who ate Roger Williams?"[110]

If you read the historical account, it tells about how an apple tree was planted above and possibly to mark the grave of Roger Williams -- a prominent figure in the 1600s and important in the history of Rhode Island. The apple tree grew and spread its roots down into the grave, drawing its nourishment from the decaying body and bones of Roger Williams. Upon exhumation for reburial, very little bone could be found -- only the tree root[111] that had entered the coffin and followed the path of his decomposing bones was prominently displayed. In fact, the roots retained some of his shape -- curved where his head should have been, growing down his spine, branching[112] at the two legs and then upturned into feet! As the tree produced fruit, the nutrients and particles from Roger Williams' body were undoubtedly now a part of the fruit. When apples from the tree were eaten, the molecules that the tree used to produce those apples were obviously part of the nutrients that came from Roger Williams' decaying body. So now it appears that every being that consumed any apples from that tree also ingested molecules from Roger Williams' body and those

---

[110] Roger Williams 1603-1683, public domain.

[111] This is a public domain nineteenth century picture of the Roger Williams Root now in the collection of the Rhode Island Historical Society.
http://en.wikipedia.org/wiki/File:Roger_Williams_Root.jpg

molecules were now part of their bodies!

Do you see the enormity of the resurrection? God will bring all of that together again. He will put the body back together and reunite it with the spirit.

Matthew 10:28 is one final passage on this subject. It says, "And do not fear those who can kill the body, but are unable to kill the soul; but rather fear Him who is able to destroy both soul and body in hell. The writer of this Scripture, Matthew, was careful to include the word "body" in the context of destroying the soul. He could have said, "Do not fear him who can kill the body; fear him who can kill the soul." But instead, he included the word "body" along with the word "soul." So it seems that as one considers this passage and the ones previously mentioned, bodies are important to God.

THE BODY IS NOT SINFUL

It should be noted that sin is not a bodily entity. It is not a physical thing. Some people think that when we go to heaven, sin will just "fall off" on the way there. But sin is not a bodily thing.

In the New International Version, 1 Corinthians 6:18 says, "Flee from sexual immorality. All other sins a man commits are outside his body, but he who sins sexually sins against his own body." The word other is in italics in the New American Standard Version because it isn't in the original Greek. Though translators have taken the liberty of inserting it, the word "other" is not part of the Greek manuscript. The Scripture is not talking about other sins, it is saying that sin is something outside of the body, but you can sin against your own body. Our body is not sinful; our nature is sinful. The body, in itself, is not sinful, but it can be a vehicle for sin.

The New Living Translation translates the verse, "Run away from sexual sin! No other sin so clearly affects the body as this one does. For sexual immorality is a sin against your own body." This version does a better job of communicating the idea of turning sin against one's body, where the body bears the consequences for the sin -- even though it is not sinful.

There is nothing wrong with a body. How do we know that? For one thing, Jesus had a body. When Adam and Eve were first created, they had perfect bodies. God now has a body.

The picture[113] depicts Thomas (John 20:27) putting his hand into the gash where the solder pierced Christ's side while on the cross. Christ had a real body and yet was sinless.

Genesis 18 - 19 is a good support for the fact that the body is not sinful. Three men appeared to Abraham. The Bible says, "The Lord appeared [theophany] . . . to Abraham . . . he suddenly noticed three men standing nearby. He got up and ran to meet them, welcoming them by bowing low to the ground . . . he took some cheese curds and milk and the roasted meat, and he served it to the men. As they ate, Abraham waited on them." It goes on to say that the two other men went on toward Sodom, but the Lord remained with Abraham (18:22).

The Bible says that Abraham bowed to them.[114] He treated them like royalty. He knew that one was the Lord. He washed their feet. They had REAL feet and toes! They rested. They ate. They refreshed themselves.

When Abraham offered them food, why didn't they say, "No, we don't have real bodies, so we don't need to eat"? They ate the food, so

---

[113] This vintage engraving depicts Jesus Christ appearing to the Apostles after the Resurrection. Saint Thomas touches the wound, removing any doubt he has that Christ has risen. This dramatic scene from the Bible was engraved after the artwork of Alexander Bida (1813 - 1895). It was published in an 1875 collection of artwork featuring Christ and is now in the public domain.

[114]Picture of Abraham and the Three Angels by Loggia di Raffaello (Vatican, 1517-1519) (Public Domain)

they must have had real stomachs.

In the next chapter (19) the Bible changes the way it refers to the two men and states that they are angels. When Lot saw them, he bowed and offered to wash their feet. Again, they had REAL feet. The men of the city lusted after them. They must have had real bodies since it is improbable that the men of Sodom lusted after spirits. The angels must have also had good-looking bodies since the men of the city asked for them to have sex with them.

So here you have God, two angels, Abraham, and Lot all in bodies. Where did God and the angels get their bodies? Are there bodies hanging up in heaven, waiting to be taken on for such purposes? Were bodies created for this special purpose? We are not told. But this passage demonstrates that bodies are not sinful.

In the previous section, the reference was made to Acts 7:55-56 and Matthew 10:28, showing the importance of bodies to God. But the same passages also demonstrate that bodies are not sinful. Consider the passages again. Matthew 10:28 says, "And do not fear those who can kill the body, but are unable to kill the soul; but rather fear him who is able to destroy both soul and body in hell." "Look," Stephen said in Acts 7:55-56, "I see heaven open and the Son of Man standing at the right hand of God." Remember, the term "son of man" means "having the characteristics of man." In other words, he saw God in a body.

So the body is not sinful, but it can be a vehicle for sin. This author does not believe that there is a gene or chromosome for the sin nature. The sins of Adam and Eve are carried down through the generations; therefore, sin is part of our spiritual nature. It is an aspect of our nature -- not our body.

A BETTER DEFINITION OF PERSON

When seeking the proper definition of "person," the necessity of starting with God and not with us has already been established because, as was stated earlier, most of the time when we start with us, we think of "person" as a human being. All human beings are persons, but not all persons are human beings.

The best definition of a person is "anyone who is like God." The Bible makes it clear that God is a person or a "personal being." It is this author's belief that angels are also persons because they are called the "sons of God" in Job 1:6. In other words, angels have the characteristics of God in the same way that humans do. (Though I believe that angels are in the image and likeness of God, the Scripture does not tell us that -- mainly because it is relatively silent about angels. It doesn't even directly tell us when they were created.) Satan is referred to as a person in Job 1:7. Satan is a fallen angel, so he is a person. We know that human beings are made in the image and likeness of God from Genesis 1: 26, 27.

Look at Genesis 18-19 again. It is a good text to show all three persons -- humans, angels, and God -- in one place at one time. Three men come to visit Abraham and we find out later in the story that they are two angels and "the Lord." So here you have a story with three different kinds of "persons" (man, angels, and God) all conversing with each other -- thinking, behaving, interacting, and communicating.

Image and Likeness

Human beings are persons because we are like God. How do we know we are like God? There are six passages found in Scripture that tell that we are created in His image and likeness.

1) Genesis 1:26 says, "Let us make man in Our image, according to Our likeness; and let them rule over the fish of the sea and over the birds of the sky and over the cattle and over all the earth, and over every creeping thing that creeps on the earth."

2) Genesis 1:27 goes on to say, "And God Created Man in His own image, in the image of God, He created him; male and female He created them."

3) Genesis 5:1 says, "He made him in the likeness of God."

4) Genesis 9:6 -- ". . . For in the image of God, He made man."

5) 1 Corinthians 11:7 -- "For a man ought not to have his head covered, since he is in the image and glory of God. . . ."

6) James 3:9 -- ". . . men, who have been made in the likeness of God."

Three Views of the Human Makeup

When reading passages in the Bible about man, many times distinctions seem to be made between the physical part of our being and the nonphysical part. Understanding what the Bible says about man cannot be done without noting those passages that appear to refer to that immaterial part, including the numerous passages that mention the "soul" and/or the "spirit." People who make a distinction between the physical part of man and the nonphysical part are either "dichotomists" or trichotomists." Others, who would say that we (human beings) are merely physical and the part that appears to be nonphysical (the mind) is simply an outworking of the brain, are referred to as "monists."

So what category would you put yourself in? Are you a trichotomist? A dichotomist? A monist? Does it really matter? This author believes it does. As you read the following discussions of each category, see if you can determine why.

MONISM

Monists: body/physical only; soul/spirit = the mind -- an outworking of the brain/body. Monists believe that there is no dichotomy -- that we, as humans, are just a physical entity and the brain is a part of that physical entity. We are physical only. There is nothing spiritual that is a separate entity. Anything "spiritual" would simply be an outworking of the brain.

There are Christian theorists such as David Meyer and Malcolm Jeeves, who hold to a monistic position. In their book, *Psychology through the Eyes of Faith*, they use science to show that we are only brains and there is no dichotomy. They say that any passage in the Bible that uses the term "soul" or "spirit" is just the biblical author's way of trying to explain the mind (synapses firing in the brain).

Their belief is that when the brain is dead, the body is dead and there is no spirit or soul.

The person is nonexistent after death, but put back into existence again at the resurrection. The resurrection brings him back to life and brings his brain back to life. Even though a person may have been dead for 2,000 years, his renewal would seem instantaneous. They would say that when 2 Corinthians 5:8 says, ". . . we would prefer to be away from the body and at home with the Lord," Paul is talking about an illusion that will "seem" instantaneous, even though it won't be.

The problem with that idea involves the inspiration of Scripture. If Scripture says that there is a soul/spirit, then I do not believe that we should explain it away because of our assumptions based upon the current research. (This goes back to the Two-Book View. It is this author's belief that they are letting research dictate what the Bible is saying.)

VERSES THAT SHOW WE ARE MORE THAN "JUST BRAINS" – MORE THAN ONE PART – REFUTING MONISM

A number of scriptural passages seem to discount the theory of monism. The following are some of them. 1 Samuel 28:1-20; Luke 16:19-31; Luke 23:46; Matthew 10:28, 26:41; Philippians 1:24; 2 Corinthians 5:9, 7:1; and James 2:26.

In the 1 Samuel passage, Samuel was already dead. Saul was preparing

to do battle with the Philistines and he was afraid. Since God did not answer his prayers, he became desperate to know what to do and how to be successful in the battle. So he sought a medium, even though he had required that all of the mediums be removed from the land. The NIV (New International Version) Bible records the medium as saying, "I see a *spirit* coming up out of the ground." [115]

How do monists explain that story? If they say, "It's just a story," then I have a problem with their view of the doctrine of inspiration of Scriptures. If it is recorded in the Bible as a true story, then monism is not

---

[115] Picture of Saul with medium and Samuel -- English: The Shade of Samuel Invoked by Saul Русский: Аэндорская волшебница вызывает тень пророка Самуила Date; 1857 Author; D. Martynov (1826-1889) *This image (or other media file) is in the public domain because its copyright has expired.*
http://commons.wikimedia.org/wiki/File:Witch_of_Endor_%28Martynov%29.jpg

a viable option.

Luke 16:19-31 tells the story of the rich man and Lazarus. One was with Abraham and the other was in torment. (Some have explained the place of torment as being the lower part of Sheol.) Both died; but after death they were men talking, thinking, experiencing emotions -- even though their bodies (and brains) had died.

The passage seems to assume their personhood/spirituality. Some people say that conclusions about that kind of theology can't be drawn from the parable. But we CAN draw something from parables. God told us things that COULD HAVE happened. If it never could happen, then there would be no basis for reality.

Luke 23:46 says, "Jesus called out with a loud voice, 'Father, into your hands I commit my spirit.' When he had said this, he breathed his last." When the spirit left, Christ's organs stopped. If we are merely brains and neurons, why is it that when the neurons stop firing, the spirit is gone? And why wouldn't it say that the spirit "died" rather than "left"? The wording implies that there is an entity that is separate from the body that moves on, to exist in another place, rather than to cease existing for a period of time.

Matthew 10:28 says, "Do not be afraid of those who kill the body but cannot kill the soul. Rather, be afraid of the One who can destroy both soul and body in hell."

Matthew 26:41 -- "Watch and pray so that you will not fall into temptation. The spirit is willing, but the body is weak."

Philippians 1:24 -- "but it is more necessary for you that I remain in the body."

2 Corinthians 5:9 -- "So we make it our goal to please him, whether we are at home in the body or away from it."

2 Corinthians 7:1 -- "Since we have these promises, dear friends, let us purify ourselves from everything that contaminates body and spirit, perfecting holiness out of reverence for God."

James 2:26 -- "As the body without the spirit is dead, so faith without deeds is dead."

In light of the preceding verses, it seems evident that Scripture teaches there is a spiritual entity separate from the body. One can see that monism is hard to substantiate biblically.

DICHOTOMY

DEFINITION

Dichotomy: body and soul/spirit -- material and immaterial. The dichotomists believe that man has two entities. They see him as made up of two parts, a dichotomy -- of material (body) and immaterial (soul/spirit). There is no distinction in essence between the soul and the spirit. It is considered one part. The body is considered the other part.

BIBLICAL DATA: SOUL AND SPIRIT

Either Term Can Refer to the Whole Immaterial Part

Matthew 10:28 says, "Do not be afraid of those who kill the body but cannot kill the soul. Rather, be afraid of the One who can destroy both soul and body in hell." In this passage, the word, "soul" is used for the immaterial part. The passage is telling us that we should fear only the ones who can kill ALL of our being, not just our body.

1 Corinthians 7:34 -- "and his interests are divided. An unmarried woman or virgin is concerned about the Lord's affairs: Her aim is to be devoted to the Lord in both body and spirit. But a married woman is concerned about the affairs of this world -- how she can please her husband."

In this passage, the word, "spirit," is used for the immaterial part. The verse is saying that she can be WHOLLY committed to the Lord -- in body and spirit. It's not saying that 2/3 of her will be committed. The word for soul is "psuche" and the word for spirit is "pneuma." Both words refer to the same entity -- the WHOLE immaterial part.

Either term can refer to the disembodied, immaterial person.

Either term (soul or spirit) can refer to the disembodied immaterial person -- that is, the immaterial person without a body. Hebrews 12:23 talks about the spirits of righteous men in heaven, whereas Revelation 6:9 talks about the souls of those martyrs who were slain and are now in heaven. Again, the terms are used interchangeably.

Hebrews 12:23 -- ". . .You have come to God himself, who is the judge of all people. And you have come to the spirits of the redeemed in heaven who have now been made perfect" (New Living Translation). (The NIV says, "the spirits of righteous men made perfect.") They are called spirits and they are already in heaven!

Revelation 6:9 -- "And when the Lamb broke the fifth seal, I saw under the altar the souls of all who had been martyred for the word of God and for being faithful in their witness" (New Living Translation). It says he *saw the souls* of all who had been martyred!

One place refers to them as spirits. Another refers to them as souls. Both refer to the disembodied immaterial persons. Maybe with perfected eyes, we will be able to see souls/spirits. Man is still a localized entity, but he IS a spirit. It is this author's position that God uses the two words -- soul and spirit -- to give a different description of the same part (since the words can have slightly different meanings). This author believes that man consists of two parts, the body and the soul/spirit -- the material and the immaterial.

TRICHOTOMY
CLASSIFICATION DETAILS

Lastly, there are those that believe that there are three separate components: the body, the soul, and the spirit. This view is appropriately called "trichotomy." The true trichotomists believe that man is made up of body, soul (psychological part that has to do with humans), and spirit (the spiritual part that has to do with God).

A trichotomy position is typically supported with one passage, that being 1 Thessalonians 5:23 where it says, "May God himself, the God of peace, sanctify you through and through. May your whole spirit, soul, and body be kept blameless at the coming of our Lord Jesus Christ." It sounds like three entities are there. But take a look at the data.

SCRIPTURAL INFORMATION SHEDDING LIGHT ON TRICHOTOMY VIEW

Trichotomy is based upon a separate listing of the terms. The verse that was just mentioned (1 Thessalonians 5:23) lists each of the terms separately -- spirit, soul, and body. But a separate listing does not always mean separate parts.

What about Mark 12:30? It reads: "Love the Lord you God with all your heart and with all your soul and with all your mind and with all your strength." Are we now quadrachotomists?

Matthew 22:37 -- "Jesus replied: 'Love the Lord your God with all your heart and with all your soul and with all your mind.'" What happened to "strength" in that passage?

Deuteronomy 6:5 -- "Love the Lord your God with all your heart and with all your soul and with all your strength." What happened to mind? So, which is it, mind or strength?

The point being made here is, "Love God with ALL OF YOU!" God doesn't appear to be telling us that there are three or four distinct parts! Many unique labels are used in Scripture to identify the inner/nonphysical part of man. This vital indicator of man can be characterized of the same person by terms such as: soul, spirit, heart, mind, will, bowels, etc.

Bowels? Yes. The Bible talks about "bowels of compassion" in   1

John 3:17, and it says "my bowels are troubled" in Lamentations 1:20 (King James Version). In Lamentations 2:11 it says, "my bowels are troubled, my liver is poured upon the earth" (KJV). Even the "liver" is mentioned here. Numerous verses refer to loving God with all of your "heart." The heart is an organ that pumps blood!

These verses are merely referring to the deepest part of man. When it says, "bowels of compassion," it is saying to be compassionate in your deepest parts. -- Bowels are pretty deep! These are not separate parts, but functions of one essence.

CONCLUSION OF 3 VIEWS OF HUMAN MAKEUP

The key point when considering any of the three views of human makeup is to remember that whenever we view humans, we need to remain holistic. Man has different aspects, but they all work together to create one person. The parts are integrally related so that the soul/spirit profoundly affects the body and the body profoundly affects the soul/spirit. Sometimes the parts appear to be indistinguishable. Though it can be helpful to divide in order to understand, no matter what position is taken -- monism, dichotomy, or trichotomy -- in reality, our problems can only be understood as we put together the material with the immaterial. Each can affect the other. Yet all of the parts are really working together as one.

Biblical Data Regarding the Soul or Spirit

In order to grasp how we function as humans, it is important to take a look at the immaterial ("psychological") part of man. The Bible has a plethora of information to help us understand ourselves, to understand others, and to know how to live in our world. The words in the Bible for "soul" and "spirit" are key words to study when seeking to learn what the Bible has to say about the "psychological" part of man. The next section will examine the terms *soul* and *spirit* as they are used in the Bible.

BIBLICAL USAGE OF TERMS FOR "SOUL" -- "NEPHESH"/"PSUCHE"

The Hebrew word *nephesh* and the Greek word *psuche"* are the words that mean *soul* in the languages used by the biblical writers. The Old Testament was written primarily in Hebrew, thus the word *nephesh* was used. The original language of the writings in the New Testament was Greek, thus the use of the word *psuche*. In the Bible, *soul* is used in different contexts to mean different things. It has four main usages. 1. **Person** is the most common usage for the term *soul*. 2. **Life or breath** is another usage. 3. **Heart and mind** are the words that current translators use when the word *soul* depicts the emotional/intellectual part of man. 4. **Either "part" only** is another way the word *soul* is used, meaning either the material part -- referring to the body aspect, or the immaterial part – non-body aspect.

1. SOUL = PERSON

When the word *soul* is used in the Bible, it often means "person." "Person" is the most common usage for the term, *soul*. The following verses illustrate that usage.

Genesis 17:14 -- ". . . that soul shall be cut off from his people" (KJV). Are they just cutting out his immaterial part? No. It is referring to a person.

Numbers 31:28 -- "one soul of 500" (KJV)

Acts 2:43 -- ". . . fear came upon every soul" (KJV). [116]

Acts 3:23 -- ". . . every soul who does not heed that prophet shall be utterly destroyed from among the people" (NASB).

All of the verses above

---

[116] Image found in public domain at: http://atonementparish.blogspot.com/ Picture of "souls" being filled with Holy Spirit at Pentecost (Accessed 3/12/09).

demonstrate how the word *soul* refers to a person. Even in our current day, we still use the word *soul* that way. We say there were three "souls" saved, when we are referring to three persons. When we use the word *soul* in that context, we are not saying that we watched the immaterial part walk down the aisle! When we say, "Not a 'soul' was around," we mean, "Not a 'person.'"

Another evidence in the Bible where the word "soul" refers to a person, is the fact that the personal pronoun is used for "soul" -- the pronoun "he/she."[117] Also "soul" is used in reference to God in Jeremiah 6:8 when He says, ". . . lest my soul depart from thee" (KJV) and again in Jeremiah 9:9 -- ". . . shall not my soul be avenged. . ." (KJV). (God, here, is the person being referred to by the pronoun "my.")

In summary, the Bible more commonly refers to man *being* a soul (man IS a soul) rather than *having* a soul, because the main usage of the word "soul" refers to the "whole person."

2. SOUL = LIFE OR BREATH

Animals have a "life principle." Do they have a soul? Do insects have a soul? When a fly[118] goes buzzing around your head and you go "clap!" he's dead. You've killed the "life principle." Did his "soul" depart from his body?

Man also has a "life principle" -- though it is attached to his "immaterial" part.

---

[117] Floyd E. Hayes, "Biblical Definitions," *Religion*, Homepage last updated on 29 December 2008 http://www.geocities.com/floyd_hayes/religion_death1 (12 March 2009).

[118] Fly picture from http://karenswhimsy.com/public-domain-images/insects/insects-4.shtm.

Genesis 2:7 -- "He breathed into his nostrils the breath of life, and the man became a living being (soul)."[119] If you are not breathing, you're dead! The life principle is gone.

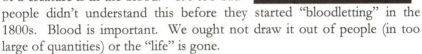

Exodus 4:19 -- ". . . all the men are dead which sought thy life (soul)" (KJV). "Soul" equals the life principle.

Leviticus 17:11 -- "For the life (soul) of a creature is in the blood." It's too bad people didn't understand this before they started "bloodletting" in the 1800s. Blood is important. We ought not draw it out of people (in too large of quantities) or the "life" is gone.

In all of these passages, "soul" refers to the characteristic of "living."

3. SOUL = HEART/MIND

The word *soul* is also used to identify the emotional/intellectual aspect of man.

1 Samuel 2:33 -- "to grieve your heart (soul)"

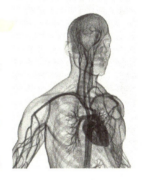

Proverbs 23:7 -- "For as he thinketh in his heart (soul) (translated in NASB "within himself"), so is he" (KJV).

Ephesians 6:6 -- ". . . doing the will of God

---

from the heart (soul)."

The previous verses may cause one to wonder, "Where are the emotions?" Are they in the heart? Are they in the brain?[120] What if a heart transplant was performed? Would the emotions from one person be transplanted to another? What if I get "butterflies" in my stomach. Is my stomach where my emotions are?

4. SOUL = EITHER PART (MATERIAL OR IMMATERIAL)

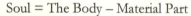

Soul = The Body – Material Part

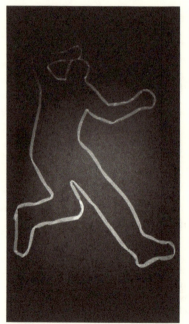

In Numbers 19:13, the people are instructed not to touch any dead bodies (souls).[121] Dead bodies are souls! A body without ANYTHING immaterial is called a "soul."

Leviticus 21:11 -- "He must not enter a place where there is a dead body (soul)" (NIV). "He must never defile himself by going near a dead person (soul)" (New Living Translation).

Numbers 6:6 -- "He must not go near a dead body (soul)" (NIV). "He shall not go near to a dead person (soul)" (NASB).

Haggai 2:13 -- "Then Haggai said, 'If a person defiled by contact with a dead body (soul) touches one of these things, does it become defiled?'"

---

[120] Picture from http://healinglightseries.com/IMAGES/Images-Heart/Brain2.jpg (16 March 2009).

[121] Body outline picture from http://www.publicdomainpictures.net/view-image.php?image=5382&picture=dead-body-outline&large=1

Soul = The Immaterial Part

Matthew 10:28 refers again to not fearing those who can kill the body, but those "who can destroy both body and soul in hell."

Revelation 6:9 -- ". . . the souls of those who had been slain because of the word of God."

Psalm 63 says, "O God, you are my God. Earnestly, I seek you. My soul thirsts for you. My body longs for you, in a dry and weary land where there is no water." It says, "body" and "soul" -- all of me. My "soul" thirsts for you. "My body longs for you." Here "soul" is used as the entire immaterial part of man.

CONCLUSION OF BIBLICAL USAGE OF TERMS FOR SOUL

If I'm talking about the "soul," what is the key? I have to understand the context! The interpretation depends on the context and must be understood in context.

So here is what we are saying about soul. When the term for "soul" (*nephesh* or *psuche*) is used in the Bible, it can be the "whole person," the "immaterial part" alone, or it can be the "body" alone. It can be both, one, or the other -- depending on the context. And it can mean "life and breath" as well.

So, when someone says to you, "Well, 'soul' is your 'psychological' part," biblically speaking, that doesn't work. Because, it *could be* the psychological part, depending on how you are referring to "psychological." But it *may not be*. It could also be the body by itself -- the material part. It could be the whole person. (Most of the time it is used that way.) Or it could simply be the "life principle."

The "bottom line" is, when people say, "The body is the physical part, the soul is the psychological part, and the spirit is the spiritual part. When you have a problem with the body, you go to a physician. If you have a problem with the soul, you go to a psychologist or counselor. And if you have a spiritual problem, you go to a pastor," they are conjecturing about something that is not supported by the terminology used in Scripture. It doesn't work biblically, even though it might sound good. The term "soul" can only be precisely understood by taking into account the context in which it was used.

BIBLICAL USAGE OF TERMS FOR SPIRIT

The term, *spirit*, is a little different than *soul*, in terms of usages. What is interesting is that the term *spirit* (*ruak* in Hebrew and *pneuma* in Greek) is *never used for the body alone*. It is *not used for the whole person* -- body plus immaterial part -- so there is a notable difference in the way the word "spirit" is used, biblically, as compared to the word *soul*. Yet one would still need to look at the context sometimes to understand the intended meaning.

There are three usages for the term *spirit*. The first one, 1) "Life or Breath," has only one verse to support it. We'll look at that. The second one, 2) "Heart or Mind," involves that emotional, intellectual part again. And, the third one, 3) "The Immaterial Part" is different and distinct from the body.

1. SPIRIT = "LIFE PRINCIPLE"

The first of the usages for the term, *spirit* is represented by only one verse, Revelation 13:15, which says, "He was given power to give breath to the image of the first beast." In the artist's image of the beast, [122] notice it has a "life principle."

Antichrist depicted as a beast with seven heads by Matthias Gerung (1500-1570)

---

[122]http://other-voices.net/weird-beliefs.html. (Public domain because of age of picture.)

2. SPIRIT = HEART OR MIND

Secondly, *spirit* can equal "heart or mind," the emotional/intellectual aspect. It can refer to the "thinking" part of us or the "feeling" part of us.

Exodus 28:3 says ". . . whom I have endowed with the spirit of wisdom" (NASB). In this verse, the word "spirit" is referring to that intellectual part of man. "Mind" might be another word that would fit the translation -- that "mind" of wisdom.

Genesis 41:8 is referring to Pharaoh when it says, "His spirit was troubled, so he sent and called for all the magicians of Egypt, and all its wise men" (NASB). (NIV says, "His mind was troubled.") *Spirit* here is referring to a "feeling" part of Pharaoh.

Pharaoh[123] had his own counselors. They were the magicians and other wise men of Egypt. So they came to try to comfort him.

But his spirit was troubled -- his "emotional" part was disturbed. It appears from the biblical data that our emotions and our intellect are housed in the "spirit." And yet our brain works and that is part of the body. So there you have your *mind*, which is affected by your *body*, of which the *brain* is a part, with which your *spirit* functions. You have a "mind/body/spirit/brain"kind of thing going. Scripture seems to be saying here that the nonmaterial, spiritual part of man is all tied in with the emotional, intellectual parts. The spirit is a nonmaterial part of us, and yet, when man is living, it is vitally connected to those neurons firing.

---

[123] Picture of pharaoh from
http://www.searchingthescriptures.net/main_pages/free_bible_clip-art.htm#Joseph Free Bible Clipart available in the public domain.

3. SPIRIT = THE IMMATERIAL "PART"

The word *spirit* can refer to the entire immaterial part of man that is distinct from the body.

Numbers 16:22 -- "O God, God of the spirits of all mankind . . ."

Psalm 51:10 -- ". . . renew a steadfast spirit within me."

1 Corinthians 7:34 -- "Her aim is to be devoted to the Lord in both body and spirit."

Hebrews 12:23 -- "You have come . . . to the spirits of righteous men made perfect."

As was stated previously, the word *spirit* is never used for the physical alone as *soul* sometimes is. The "spirit" does seem to be a major aspect of personhood. God, angels, and Satan (being a fallen angel) are spirits and human beings have spirits. They all are spirit beings.

CONCLUSION OF SOUL/SPIRIT

DISTINCTION BETWEEN "SOULISH" AND "SPIRITISH"

1 Corinthians 15:44 says, "it is sown a natural body, it is raised a spiritual body. If there is a natural body, there is also a spiritual body." Notice the "it" in both phrases is the same essence. The verse is talking about two forms of one's body-- one is natural, one is spiritual. The "it" in both phrases refers to the body. But that body can be adapted for spiritual/heavenly purposes or for earthly purposes. And in this passage, when it is talking about earthly purposes, it is actually the term, *soul* that is used. When it says, "It is sown a natural body," it is really translated, according to the Greek, a "soulish" body. If it is adapted for heavenly things, the translation then is that it is a "spiritual" body. If we are going to make a distinction, the natural/earthly body is more "soulish" and the heavenly body is more "spiritish" -- that is, if you *have to* make a distinction. Essentially, though, it is the same essence, with different functions.

One day, our bodies are going to be adapted for heaven. And we are going to have, according to 1 Corinthians 15:44, spiritual bodies. But right now, our bodies are adapted for the earth. Our bodies are more natural or "soulish" bodies. But whether for heaven or earth, each of us will be the same person with the same body.

So, when people say, "Well, our 'spirit' is what talks to God and our 'soul' is what talks to each other," there's a little bit of truth to that. If one is using the word *soul*, it would have to do more with earthly kinds of things, and *spirit* would have more to do with heavenly things.

But here is the key. It is the same IT! Soul and spirit are the same essence! It is not like there are two distinct entities. (We are just talking about function now.)

It is the same with the body. Sometimes it is adapted for earthly things and sometimes it is adapted for heavenly things; but it's the same body.

Hebrews 4:12 may help to clarify this a little. It says, "For the word of God is living and active. Sharper than any double-edged sword, it penetrates even to dividing soul and spirit, joints and marrow: it judges the thoughts and attitudes of the heart."

The word of God is SO SHARP, it can slice through soul and spirit! It can even make a distinction between the soul and the spirit.

There are some who look at this verse and say, "See, spirit and soul are distinctly separate." And some use this verse to defend the dividing up of man's immaterial entities -- promoting the thinking that we have both a "soul" and a "spirit." They assume that this verse means there are two distinct entities. But if soul and spirit are two distinct entities, does it take a really sharp object to divide them? If the terms are distinct, would it take the word of God to divide that? No.

But if it is the same "it" (soul/spirit) and it is a slightly different function, now Hebrews 4:12 makes sense. The word of God is so sharp it can even make that unfathomable distinction! So those who use Hebrews 4:12 to defend the trichotomist view may want to look again and consider whether it may be a better support of the dichotomist position.

Even 1 Thessalonians 5:23, which says, "May your whole spirit, soul, and body be kept blameless at the coming of our Lord Jesus Christ," appears to be only making the point that the desire is that "all of you" be kept blameless. (This was discussed previously.) Paul is saying, "May *all of you* be sanctified," in the same way that loving the Lord your God with all of your heart, soul, and mind (Matt. 22:37) means loving Him with *all of you*.

A number of hymns and praise songs declare many of these aspects. One praise song expresses that we "Love the Lord" with our mind, and spirit, and soul, and will, etc., and every verse uses a different word. Does that mean that we are now quintichotomists? Do we have many parts to us? No! We are just saying "all of us."

So, the key phrase summarizing the soul/spirit is: "One immaterial essence with differing functions."   And that immaterial essence is intertwined with the material/bodily essence.

IMMATERIAL INTERTWINED WITH MATERIAL

Looking at the body and the immaterial part -- the body and spirit -- is like examining a tapestry. The tapestry is woven together. It is not like two pieces "stuck" together (kind of "glued") and at death one sort of "breaks off." The soul/spirit is more like a tapestry, intricately woven with our body in a way that really cannot be unraveled until death.

Sometimes we have physical problems that affect our spirits, and sometimes we have spiritual problems that affect our bodies. All of those aspects can work hand-in-hand. It is important to remember that. Our theology dictates that we are holistic beings.

"Well, your problem is a 'spiritual' problem." That could be. But our theology also says that it could be a 'body' problem that is affecting your spirit.

As a student of Christian psychology, challenge yourself to do word studies on *soul* and *spirit*. Use some of the tools that are now readily available in libraries or on the Internet and find out what the Bible says about the words *soul* and *spirit*. What do they mean? How is each word used in the Bible? If you do a word study, you may find that *body* and *soul* and *spirit* may not be as easily diagramed as some try to do in order to make sense of them all.

Rather than starting with our own preconceived ideas, let's start with the biblical data and then let that bring our theory into being. That is what is most important.

FINAL THOUGHTS ON "SOUL/SPIRIT"

So, if you were asked right now, "What is the conclusion about 'soul/spirit?'" what would you say? One conclusion would be that, though there are three usages for "spirit" and four usages for "soul," context is a key for both of them.

But pulling it all together, *the soul/spirit is one immaterial essence with differing functions.* In other words, we have a material part of us called the "body," which is intertwined with an immaterial part of us -- our "soul/spirit" -- that is one essence. Sometimes that essence is called "soul." Sometimes it is called "spirit." Call it "soul/spirit." It is one essence. Thus, this book promotes the dichotomist view, seeing two distinct elements.

CHAPTER 4

PERSONALITY: PART 2

When Does Personhood Begin?

INTRODUCTION

Now, to direct our study to another subject, it is time to look at the inception of personhood. Where does personhood begin? Do you think that is an important question? Is it critical for me, as a Christian, to know where I stand on this issue of personhood? Will my view affect my daily life?

In the famous 1973, "Roe V. Wade" case, the Supreme Court left open the definition of what a person is, and the Supreme Court's ruling stated that "it could not resolve the difficult question of when life begins." It stated that ". . . The judiciary . . . is not in a position to speculate as to the answer." And then admitted, "If this suggestion of personhood is established, the appellant's case [i.e., "Roe" who sought an abortion], of course, collapses, for the fetus' right to life is then guaranteed specifically by the (14th) Amendment." The court made this statement regarding the openness to overruling their decision because they felt that there could be a time in the future where science could prove that personhood was established at a particular point in gestation that was different from the point in time currently accepted. (Notice that "science" is the measuring stick for personhood. The Supreme Court was, however, acknowledging the point that was made in these writings, that science is fallible/changeable and the grounds on which their decision was based in 1973 may be viewed differently in the future.) So the Supreme Court left the definition of personhood open to future discussion and rulings.

In the fall of 2006, a bill was introduced in Congress called the "Life at Conception Act." The bill declared unborn children "persons" and stated that that they are "entitled to legal protection." Declaring unborn fetuses "persons" would give them the rights of U.S. citizens, but if they are not "persons," then they do not have those rights. The bill specified that a person was distinguished as such at his/her very conception.

Though it was not passed in the 108th Congress, subsequent "Right to Life" acts have continued to be introduced. The definition of personhood and when it begins is something that is openly debated in the very top courts of our country. So it is a very important point for us to consider as well. We have already defined what personhood is. Now our study will focus on the question: When does personhood begin?

Knowing the answer to that question is part of our theology! "When does that group of cells become a person?" When do persons become persons? The following are differing views.

OVERVIEW OF THE THREE THEORIES OF
THE ORIGIN OF PERSONS

Examined here will be three theories that presume the origin of persons.

1) The first one is the Pre-Existence Theory. This theory says that there are soul/spirits "up there," somewhere, waiting for bodies to form naturally.

2) The Creation Theory is the second one we will examine. It says that God creates spirits every time men and women come together sexually resulting in the formation of a zygote. Whenever an egg is fertilized, a spirit is created by God and placed in a naturally made body.

3) The final theory -- the Traducian Theory -- says, "No! Soul/Spirits aren't up there floating around. And no, God doesn't create new spirits every time an egg is fertilized!" The Traducian Theory says, "Spirits happen naturally, just like bodies do."

As the three different theories are explained, be thinking about what can be deduced from Scripture that bears light on these theories. What can we take in our attempt to form our theology?

1. THE PRE-EXISTENCE THEORY

The Pre-Existence Theory says that there are soul/spirits "up there," somewhere, waiting for bodies to form naturally. When men and women come together sexually and a body is formed (or whenever a human egg is fertilized through any method), one of the souls/spirits that exists then inhabits the body -- thus forming a whole person. The Pre-Existence Theory assumes that the soul/spirits are already there.

In the Pre-existence Theory, basically two views are considered -- "God's Sexual Activity Forms Spirits" and "Reincarnation."

God's Sexual Activity Forms Spirit

The first view presumes that God had sex with women in heaven. Spirits are born from that union and then they wait for bodies. This is the view held by the Mormon Church. A Mormon apostle, Orson Pratt, said, "We have now clearly shown that God the Father had a plurality of wives, one or more being in eternity, by whom He begat our spirits as well as the spirit of Jesus His first born. . ."[124] "Putting this all together, Mormonism teaches the SPIRITS of all people were conceived in heaven via physical, sexual intercourse between the Father and one or more of his goddess wives. This 'heavenly sex' is possible since the Mormon god (and presumably His wives) have 'all the parts and passions' that we do."[125]

"With the teaching by the leaders of the Mormon Church that pre-existent spirits are waiting for a chance to have a human body, pressure is put on female members to bear children in order to provide these pre-existent spirits with the opportunity to have human bodies in order to fulfill the requirement that they live a mortal life in order to advance into the celestial kingdom. Utah, with a large majority of Mormons, has the highest birth rate of any state in the nation. According to Mormon theology, woman's primary purpose in life is to bear and raise children. This is partially based upon the need to provide a mortal life for pre-existent spirits. This Mormon concept is deeply rooted in Mormon history as shown by the following that appeared in *M'Clure's Magazine* in 1911 '. . . unless they come to earth, reborn, these souls are doomed to an eternal life as homeless spirit. . . Every woman is constantly surrounded by thousands, millions of them, pleading for an opportunity to get into the world.'"[126] [127]

---

[124] Jerald and Sandra Tammer, *Mormonism: Shadow or Reality?* (Salt Lake City: Utah Lighthouse Ministry, 1987), p. 227.

[125] Gary F. Zoella, *Mormonism vs. the Bible*
(http://www.dtl.org/cults/article/mormonism.htm Darkness to Light ministry (www.dtl.org) Copyright © 1999). Quote found under heading, "Sex in Heaven?" Accessed 2/20/09. The article originally appeared in *Darkness to Light* newsletter in 1994. It was posted on this Web site in July 1996.

[126] Burton Hendrick, *M'Clure's Magazine*, 1911, "The Revival of Polygamy" (Taken from The Latter Day Saints, Ruth Kauffman and Reginal Wright Kauffman, 1912).

Reincarnation

The other view is reincarnation. The Reincarnation View says that spirits were formed at some point in time. If the living person that a spirit inhabited dies, it goes somewhere and waits for another body to come around through procreation. When a new body has been formed and is available, the spirit then inhabits the new body.

How do we know from Scripture that this really isn't true? There is one verse. The best argument against reincarnation is Hebrews 9:27: "Just as man is destined to die once and after that to face judgment, so Christ was sacrificed once . . . ." We die once. We don't die several times. And do you see the problems with reincarnation? If you are a Christian in a past life but not in this one, where will you spend eternity?

From Scripture it is clear that we die once and then there is judgment. At that time, God will look at the lives of whole persons (person = body and spirit) and determine what kind of choices were made.

So the Reincarnation View can be ruled out along with the Mormon view of pre-existence.

2. THE CREATION THEORY

The "Creation Theory" says that God creates spirits every time a human male sperm penetrates a female egg, producing a body. When sexual activity takes place between a man and a woman and as a body is made through procreation, naturally, God sees that natural body and says, "I'm going to create a soul/spirit to dwell in that body." God then ACTIVELY creates a soul/spirit to indwell that body.

Of course, the next question would be, "When does God create the spirit?" Is it at conception? Or is it at eight cells? Or is it implantation? When does God create that spirit? At some point when a body is formed, God creates the spirit and both are brought together.

The "Creation Theory," or sometimes known as the "Creationist Theory," basically says that God creates spirits. And He creates them "ex

---

[127] *Spirits in the Mormon Church,* Paragraph 5, Accessed 2/20/09, http://www.mormonconspiracy.com/spirits.html Mormonconspiracy.com © 2005.

nihilo" -- "out of nothing." It is called "immediate creation." He creates spirits in the same way that He created Earth and man during first six days, "in the beginning" (Genesis 1:1).

References pertaining to this view include Zechariah 12:1, "The Lord . . . who forms the spirit of man within him . . ." He FORMED the spirit of man! It sounds like God directly creates the spirit.

How about Isaiah 57:16? ". . . for then the spirit of man would grow faint before me -- the breath of man that I have created. . ." It says, ". . . the breath of man that I have created." How did man have a "life principle" within him? God said, "I made it." Now, some would say, "Well, the spirit is the life principle."

Proponents of this view also refer to Hebrews 12:9. "Moreover, we have all had human fathers who disciplined us and we respected them for it. How much more should we submit to the Father of our spirits and live!"

Those who espouse to the Creationist Theory focus on the phrase, "the Father of spirits." They would regard God as the creator of spirits in the same way He created the world! They say that Hebrews 12:9 confirms that "God 'begat' spirits."

Considering those three passages may be enough to convince the reader that the Creation Theory is the correct view -- that God actively creates spirits whenever a new body is formed.

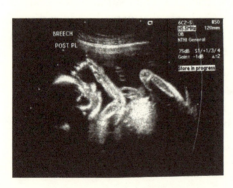

"I formed you in the womb."

Jeremiah 1:5 -- God's Laws of the Universe

But, what about Jeremiah 1:5? "Before I formed you in the womb,[128] I knew you. Before you were born I set you apart."

"Before I formed you in the womb. . ." What is God talking about? He's talking about a BODY!

---

[128] From Edgington File.

The proponents of the Creation Theory would presumably have trouble with this verse, thinking something like this: "Wait a minute! No you didn't. We can explain this scientifically. Men and women come together sexually and then there's a sperm that fertilizes an egg."

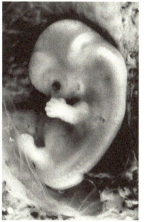

Then why does God say, "I formed you in the womb" when he is talking about bodies? God is saying, "I'm the one who put all of that in motion." Now, we are talking about "mediate" creation.

Immediate is "Ex nihilo." [129] When we use the term *Mediate*, we are talking about the laws of nature. God is the one that invented pro-creation. He is the one that put it all together, and now it can happen naturally.

That is why when things happen like a birth, we often say, "Look at the miracle!" And no physician comes in and says, "No, no! Let me explain this scientifically. It was not a miracle at all. This is what happened. . . ."

"No, it is a miracle! Look at what God made! Look what we have!" It is all true! But it happened through God's laws of how the universe works, that HE put in motion. He created that baby -- but not through immediate creation -- "Zap! Baby!" He did it through His laws -- through how He set up the universe.

Psalm 139:13-16 -- Figurative Language

How about Psalm 139:13-16? ". . . For you created my inmost being; you knit me together in my mother's womb . . . when I was made in the secret place. When I was woven together in the depths of the earth. . . ."

---

[129] Picture of 9-week old fetus on following page from Ed Uthman – Flickr.com. "My solution is to release all the specimen photos I take into the public domain, so that they may provide maximum educational benefit worldwide." Rights available at http://creativecommons.org/licenses/by/2.0. Accessed Jan 2011.

So God actually comes down and "knits" us together in the womb? No!

What is the author, David, saying here, "When you knit me together" -- "When you *formed* me"? What is David talking about when those phrases are used? It is simply figurative language for, "Look what God made through the way He set things up!" God is saying, "Yes, I made you. But Mom and Dad also made you -- naturally."

(This could also be demonstrated by the phrase, "I was woven . . . in the depths of the earth" -- v. 15. We know that David wasn't made inside the earth. He is using figurative language there.)

Now, here is the point to be made. If that is true for bodies, and that language is used . . . "God formed," "He created," "He knit," "He made," could it not also be true for spirits? Where God said, "I created your spirit, I formed your spirit, I made your spirit," could He be using figurative language there as well?

Ah! He could be talking about *mediate* creation and not *immediate* creation. There is still the body and the spirit, but it does not mean He had to go, "Zap! Spirit!"

Summary of Problems for Creationists from Jeremiah. 1:5 and Psalm 139:13-16

So, what inferences can be drawn from Jeremiah 1:5 and Psalm 139:13-16 when considering if God actively creates spirits each time a new body is formed?

1) If God directly creates spirits, if we are going to take that from Scripture, then He does it with bodies too, because the language is the same for both. Yet there is NO theologian that this author knows of that claims that God directly creates bodies. Mediate creation is assumed and accepted. To this author's knowledge, no theologian has ever said, "Yes, God directly, 'ex nihilo,' makes bodies. Bodies don't just happen through natural means." So if the language is the same for both and scholars agree that it is mediate creation for one, then it must be mediate creation for the other.

2) A distinction needs to be made between mediate and immediate creation (which we already discussed). That distinction is in regard to two types of creation. One is out of nothing, direct -- *immediate*. And the other is through God's laws that govern the universe -- *mediate*.

Other Problems for Creationists

And there are other problems that confront the Creationist -- those who say that God creates spirits directly and then puts those spirits into bodies. What about the verses that say that creation *stopped*? How did *sin* become part of the new bodies? Would the *virgin birth* be necessary?

Creation Stopped

First of all, "Immediate Creation" stopped! It tells us in Genesis 2:2 that "on the seventh day he rested from all his work." So the question to be asked would be, "Was God tired?" No. That is not what it means. What does it mean, "God rested"?

It means: He was done. He stopped. [130]

The same language is used in Exodus 20 verse 11. "In six days, God created the world and then He rested." He stopped! He is no longer creating that way today (as a general rule – Obviously God could break in and create whenever He wants, but this is not the general rule which is assumed from this passage). It is this author's belief that God is not creating new spirits every day.

God could. He has the power to. He can break in to the universe! He can do anything He wants! He is God. But I think what He is saying in those verses is, "I'm not doing that anymore with this earth. I set the

---

[130] Garden of Eden Picture from
http://clipart.christiansunite.com/1294486861/Bible_Characters_Clipart/Adam_and_Eve_Clipart/Adam_and_Eve019.jpg. ChristiansUnite free Christian Clipart. Christian images here are free for your use on web sites, newsletters, church bulletins or anywhere else you can find them useful, however redistribution is prohibited. A link to http://clipart.christiansunite.com/ would be appreciated but not mandatory if you use any of these images on a web site. Accessed 1/8/11.

world up so it would run. Now, I'm not directly creating in the way that I used to. I stopped."

Some could argue that. It may be a lot to presume all of that based on a few verses; but, it seems apparent to this author that God is saying that that type of creation ("ex nihilo") is no longer happening.

When Does Sin Become Part of the New Bodies?

Next is a bigger problem for Creation Theory advocates: What about Sin in people?

We already looked at bodies. Is there anything sinful about bodies? 1 Corinthians 6:18 says sins are "OUTSIDE his body." Sin is a "NON-BODILY" entity. All of our sins are outside of the body. Though you can sin against your body, sin is a "non-bodily" thing. Christ had a body. Adam and Eve had real bodies before the Fall and they were still perfect. We discussed that already (pp. 118-120).

So, where does sin come in? Because if bodies are good,[131] and God creates spirits to go in the bodies (the assumption being that those spirits He creates would be created perfect as well), and He puts together the bodies with the spirits, where does sin come from?

If God is directly creating spirits each time, He is not going to create a damaged or faulty spirit to put in Man. God can only create that which is good. And we have already established that bodies are not sinful. When God puts the two together (body and spirit), where does the sin come from? How do we get a sin nature?

In Psalm 51:5, it says, ". . . in SIN, did my mother conceive me!" It is not talking about the act of sex. There is nothing wrong with sex. David was saying that in his "conception," there was SIN! When fertilization happened, sin was present.

Well, how? That baby couldn't have had a thought, or made a choice, or acted sinfully.

---

[131] Though our bodies are not sinful, our human bodies bear the impact of sin. They are not "perfect" anymore -- as Adam's and Eve's bodies were. We are born with many bodily imperfections -- though those imperfections are separate from the spirit and our sinful nature.

It happened because of the baby's sin nature. We each have a sin nature. We get it naturally. The sin-inclined spirit would have to come naturally -- inherited through conception and the passing down of that sinful nature through procreation.

Well, how does the sin nature get passed down? The Bible says that by nature, we are "objects of wrath" (Ephesians 2:3). How did that happen if bodies are good and spirits are good? If you are a creationist, how do you explain sin?

About the only way that it can be explained is to say that all of us, as babies, have perfect bodies and spirits. Then, as we grow, we do like Adam and Eve -- we eventually sin. So, each individual's first sin makes him a "sinner." It starts with a thought as an infant and goes to an action -- each person eventually getting the sin nature.

But, the Bible seems to talk about a sin "nature" that is already there. So how did it get there? Some would argue, "Well, that's the way it happened for Adam and Eve! Adam and Eve were perfect and then sinned, so it can happen for everyone else the same way."

However, Romans 5 tells us that the rest of us that exist after Adam, start with a sin nature that moves to thought, that moves to action. Romans 5 tells us that we all get that sin nature naturally through one man --Adam. "Just as sin entered the world through one man, and death through sin, and in this way death came to all men . . . ." Romans 5:12. We all get a sin nature.

So the Creationists have a problem with explaining sin in people.

Would the Virgin Birth Be Necessary?

The next question and another big problem for creationists is "Would the virgin birth be necessary?" That question is crucial for the follower of the Creation Theory to address. If God "creates" a body and a spirit whenever conception occurs, then the virgin birth would be an unneeded miracle.

Consider Joseph and Mary coming together sexually and they are going to make -- according to the Creationist's view -- a body. (Remember, bodies are fine. There is nothing sinful about bodies -- p. 118-120. They are "affected" by sin, but in and of themselves they are not sinful.) Next, consider Christ who is a spirit being. (Remember, He is already a person! [p. 109]. He is the second person of the Trinity. He is already a spirit being. He doesn't have a body -- though He had a temporary body in Genesis 18 and whatever happened to that body we aren't told, but He didn't have a permanent body.) Now, the body that would have been created by Joseph and Mary would have been a perfectly good body. All that God would have had to say was, "Rather than creating a spirit, I'm going to take a spirit that's already there (Christ's spirit) and put it in this perfectly good body." Why do you have a need for a virgin birth? There is no reason or significance for it to occur.

Summary of Creation Theory Problems

So, the Creation Theory has some problems to explain -- the virgin birth, the entrance of sin, the teaching in Scripture of creation "stopping," mediate vs. immediate creation, and the figurative language contradiction.

3. THE TRADUCIAN THEORY

The last view is called the "Traducian View." The idea here is that when a man and a woman come together sexually not only is a body formed, but, very naturally, a spirit is formed as well. Bodies and spirits happen naturally.

In essence, the Traducian Theory says that when a man and woman have sexual relations and conception occurs, a WHOLE PERSON -- body AND spirit -- is generated. Genesis 5:3 -- "Adam . . . had a son in his own likeness, in his own image." The idea conveyed appears to be that this boy is not just one who looked like Adam -- although the verse could be rendered that way, but that Seth was someone that was like Adam in body and spirit.

When contrasting physical, human birth from birth as "children of God," John 1:13 says that children of God are not born the natural, human way -- ". . . children born not of natural descent, nor of human decision or of a husband's will,[132] but born of God." The natural way implies whole children -- not just bodies -- but children are born of natural descent.

And Acts 17:26: "From one man He made every nation of men." So again, these verses don't DIRECTLY teach Traducianism, but you get the idea that they are not just bodies. Persons are being formed. "Persons" descend *naturally* from Adam. Now, the virgin birth is a needed miracle.

Traducianist's View Demonstrates Need for Virgin Birth

If you are a Traducianist, the need for a virgin birth is an important factor to take into consideration. If the body and spirit are created naturally, it makes sense that the spirit which inhabits each body would "naturally" be a sinful spirit. That "natural" occurrence would explain the sin nature -- it comes naturally. It then follows that the virgin birth is now a needed miracle. But why would the virgin birth be necessary?

It is often claimed in Christian circles that the virgin birth was needed so that Christ wouldn't be sinful. But that doesn't seem to match up with what the Bible teaches, because Christ was already perfect and He was already a spirit being. What does sin have to do with it?

A very probable scenario could be that God's thinking went something like this: "If Joseph and Mary come together naturally, there is going to be created a body and a spirit. -- A person is going to be created. . ." (Let's call that person, Nathaniel.) ". . . And now we've got the second

---

[132] In fact, the word for a husband's "will" can be thought of almost as a "whim." Think about it. A guy and a girl can go, "Hey! Let's have sex!" and they can create a baby. That is something to keep in mind -- that one unplanned or "frivolous" incident can create an eternal being! That is why God takes sex very seriously. It is not that sex is BAD or that sexual sin is worse than another sin, necessarily; He's just saying that the ramifications are that we have ETERNAL creatures. And now that that person -- that whole body and spirit -- has been made, there is some responsibility that comes with that. So, God is saying, "Hey! Take sex very seriously here and treat it as something divine. Treat it as something that I gave . . . a beautiful thing. But I want it in the right context because of some of the consequences that can take place."

person of the Trinity who is going to inhabit that body. Nathaniel and Christ would be in the same body! That won't work!"

Not only would that put two people in the same body, but that bizarre situation would put a sinful spirit and a perfect spirit in the same body – a major problem! So a very plausible reason why God chose for Christ to be born of a virgin was so that there weren't two persons in one body (and one of them being sinful).

It is this author's opinion that the virgin birth was not needed to keep Christ from being sinful. It was to eliminate the other person -- the sinful spirit/person that would be created naturally and would have occupied the same body that Christ was to inhabit. God was going to get Joseph out of the picture and use Mary. Mary was a vehicle for creating a body only! Mary was the vehicle to create a body that Christ's spirit would then be fused with and take on human nature.

Christ's spirit was ready to enter the body -- a perfectly good body -- inside Mary's womb. And when the Bible says, "The spirit 'came upon' Mary," it means that the spirit was working in Mary's womb in order to say, "I'm preparing a BODY for our Lord." The Holy Spirit prepared a body that was housing a spirit being, a spirit that already existed. Christ had always been a person, but now was human being. He had never done that before.

Now, how all of that happened with the second person of the trinity -- starting with one cell, then growing into four cells and on and on; then growing in wisdom, and stature, and favor with God (Luke 2:40) -- is hard to comprehend. But the most important part to understand is that only if spirits are formed "naturally," would the virgin birth now be a NEEDED miracle. It did not happen to keep Christ from being sinful, but so that there would not be two persons in one body. God needed only one person in the body -- a sinless person. And that is where Christ's spirit entered without procreation and into the womb of a virgin -- Mary.[133]

---

[133] Another side point that may be worth touching on here is the Catholic view of Mary's perfection. Was it necessary for Mary to be perfect for "The Immaculate Conception" to occur and so that Christ was perfect? Do you see how we take our logic too far sometimes? Why would Mary have to be perfect in order for Christ to be perfect?

The idea that is presented is that you can't create a perfect body out of an imperfect person. Why not? Remember, even in procreation perfectly good bodies are made with two sinful people. But, if you start with that belief, that Mary had to be perfect so that Christ could be perfect, then you might as well keep going back. If Mary had to be perfect,

Problems Resolved with Traducianist View

So, problems with the Pre-existence Theory and the Creation Theory now seem to be resolved. The virgin birth now makes sense.

The sin nature and creation also are explained. Sin is transmitted through procreation. We inherit a sin nature. Psalm 51:5 makes sense now. Ephesians 2:3 makes sense. "We are, by nature, children of wrath." At conception, sin is present.

Creation -- immediate creation -- stopped after six days. Therefore, God is not still doing it. It all happens naturally now -- both body and spirit (physical and spiritual). Creation happens naturally. It is "mediate" as opposed to "immediate."

So defenders of this view may be thinking, "There you have it! We've solved all of the issues!" But, there is still a problem for those of us that hold this view.

When Is an Organism a Person?

When is that organism, a person? Is it eight cells? Is it four cells?[134] If it is eight cells -- then four cells is not a person? If it is four cells, then any time before that, it is not a person?

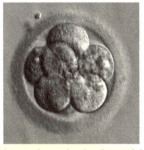

Some would say, "No. When it is a zygote or when it is an embryo then it's a person." Is it at conception? How do you know?

Some believe that personhood begins when the embryo is six days old

---

then what about her mother? Why does it stop at Mary? And that's where it gets unreasonable.

The other fact that discredits the idea that Mary was perfect is that the Bible says that Mary made a sin offering, a guilt offering (Luke 2:24 "to offer a sacrifice in keeping with what is said in the Law of the Lord: 'a pair of doves or two young pigeons.'"). She made offerings. So you get the idea that she knew that she was a sinful person that needed a savior, just like we do.

[134] Picture of Eight-Cell Embryo. This work has been released into the public domain by its author, ekem. This applies worldwide. From English Wikipedia: http://en.wikipedia.org/wiki/Image:Embryo%2C_8_cells.jpg. Accessed Jan 2011.

because God created the Earth in six days. If that were true, does that mean that when the implanted egg is five days and 23 hours old, it is not a person? So that moment that the embryo crosses that one second, then it is a person? That may be a little difficult to believe for many of us.

But based on what we have just studied, we are going to say that personhood begins at conception. When conception takes place, that fertilized egg is a person."

Where Do "Non-Implanted" Zygotes Go?

But, here is the next dilemma. Estimates report that anywhere from 30-75% of all fertilized eggs never implant in the womb and are flushed out naturally.[135] Sometimes the mother doesn't even know.

The theological question is: If those are persons (they were conceived; they just didn't implant and therefore grow and be born) -- if at conception they were persons, do they go to heaven? Do they go to hell? Or are they NOT persons?

Do they all go to heaven? Are there going to be a bunch of people in heaven that never even made it to implant in their mother's womb?

Or do you say, "No, those were all SINFUL people. The sin nature was there." So do they all go to Hell?

Where does God's grace come in? Does our sentimentality get in the way when we want all embryos and children to go to heaven? Or do

---

[135] Each of the following sites have differing estimates of lack of implantation of zygotes. They vary from 30-75%. http://kittywampus.blogspot.com/2008/10/personhood-for-zygotes.htm

http://74.125.95.132/search?q=cache:IhmUzRHwbegJ:www.babycenter.com/0_understanding-miscarriage_252.bc+%25+percent+zygote+embryo+doesn%27t+implant&cd=3&hl=en&ct=clnk&gl=us

http://74.125.95.132/search?q=cache:ZVl2R8DCvfwJ:www.illinoisivf.com/recurrent-pregnancy-loss/pre-implantation.html+%25+percent+zygote+embryo+doesn%27t+implant&cd=1&hl=en&ct=clnk&gl=us

http://74.125.95.132/search?q=cache:5NJKHVUF3kUJ:www.calvin.edu/~lhaarsma/week9.html+%25+zygote+embryo+doesn%27t+implant&cd=8&hl=en&ct=clnk&gl=us

people become too harsh and judgmental when they say, "No! If they never accepted Christ, they go to Hell"?

Wait a minute. What about abortion or babies who die in the womb? Or what about babies who die immediately after birth? Or even children who weren't old enough to make a decision, what about them?

Our theology becomes pretty important. So how do we respond to those questions? Obviously, it depends on the sovereignty of God.

One belief is that there is an "age of accountability" where, up to that age, the child is "in" -- he is going to heaven. (Christ seems to suggest something "heavenly" about children -- Matt. 19:14; Luke 18:16). But, at the point when the child becomes aware of his sin nature, that is when he is accountable.

And yet again, the same problem exists. Is it at 10 years? 11 years? Is it on one day, the person wakes up and at that point, he is at that age of accountability? Is it one particular minute or second? The problem is that nowhere is Scripture does it teach an "age of accountability."

Or does God do a special act of grace for children, who, in their innocence, are not able to think through the decision of accepting Christ? Could that be part of the nature of God?

One verse that seems to support that -- 2 Samuel 12:23. David has learned that his child that was conceived through adultery with Bathsheba has died. When questioned about the fact that he had stopped mourning, David said, "I will go to him one day" (New Living Translation). David was saying, "I will see him again."

Now, here is the important aspect of this discussion. The question is not as much personhood as it is human life.

The question of, "When is a person, a person?" may be important, based on our United States Constitution. But the more important question to be asking is, "When does a fertilized egg become human life?"

Genesis 9:6 tells us not tamper with human life. "Yes, you must execute anyone who murders another person, for to kill a person is to kill a living being made in God's image" (NLT).

It appears from that passage that God is saying, "When you know this is human life, don't tamper with it. Don't kill another living being." So rather than argue personhood and debate:

"It's 8 cells!"

"No! No! It's 16!"

"No, it's implantation."

"No, it's the 9th week."

Who knows? We can say for sure, for certain, that at conception you have human life – Human Life at Conception. So whether one concludes that there is a person at conception, or not, the one fact that is beyond debate is that human life exists at conception.

Based on our study, we will go the one step further and say, "Personhood exists at conception." And upon that principle, the subsequent writings of this book are based.

Personality in Terms of Personhood

The focus is going to shift at this point to the topic of "Personality." Why is this idea of personhood and personality so important to our study of psychology? Part of the answer lies with the reality of the discussions regarding personhood that are going on in our country (as was mentioned previously in this chapter). These issues have to do with the very theology of personality and personhood that you are being challenged to take a look at in this chapter. People are debating this in terms of the law. Our understanding of personhood and society's understanding of personhood affects what is going to happen in this country. So this is an important issue.

Another reason why the understanding of personhood and personality is so important is that it affects the way we relate to our world. "Who are we and what happens when we die?" The answer to this question affects not only the hope we have and the way we live, but it affects the messages that we communicate and the hope that we give to others. Our theology is going to come up in the way we live our lives! This is an important topic!

We have spent the bulk of the previous writings building a foundation for understanding what a person is. Now that we understand what a person is, we want to examine the question, "What is personality?"

"Personality is the name given to the nucleus of a definite group of functions,

capacities, or characteristics."[136] That is the definition that we will begin with. So what does that mean?

Our unique package of characteristics comes from both heredity and the environment. Though we are persons who have inherited a spirit and spirit beings do not have to have bodies; human beings are persons that do have bodies. Yet, persons have something called personality that is a function of the spiritual essence -- the immaterial essence, even though our bodies can affect how the immaterial essence functions.

Our personalities say something about us as persons. Personality is the way the spiritual part of us works its way out. God made us in His image as psychological/spiritual beings. Our personality reflects that image.

How does that personality reflect His image? What is the outgrowth?

To answer that, we may want to ask questions like: What are our choices? What is our thinking? How are emotions felt and expressed? What are our beliefs? What kinds of behaviors do we engage in? All of those aspects make up that psychological/spiritual part that reflects God through our personalities. We can use that psychological/spiritual part of us to serve God; or with the entrance of sin, we have new avenues to use these capacities or characteristics and many paths that we can take away from God.

A spirit being is "a metaphysical" (that is, "other than physical" or "nonmaterial") being with those functions and/or capacities that are part of personality. Therefore, if there is no spirit, there is no person -- there is no personality. The only ones who do not have personalities are the ones who don't have spirits.

So, an animal does NOT have a personality. But living creatures other than man often have something. An animal has SOMETHING. Dogs, cats, rabbits, have something that we may say is "cute," or "spunky," but it is not personality – in the strictest sense of the word.

---

[136] Theology notes, *God and Revelation*, (John Whitcomb) Grace Seminary, 1982.

THE IMAGE OF GOD

We have concluded that we are persons and have personality because we are like God. For many of us, that conclusion leads us to the realization that our personality is the essence of what it means to be made in the image of God. But, though we accept that we are like God, before we move on, it is important to take at look at how we know that from Scripture. What does the Bible have to say about man being made in His image?

As mentioned previously in this chapter, the Bible gives us only a handful of verses which talk about us being made in His image. Genesis 1:26 says, "Let us make man in our image, in our likeness, and let them rule over . . . the earth." Genesis 1:27 states, "God created man in His own image, in the image of God he created him; male and female he created them." Genesis 5:1 says, "When God created man, he made him in the likeness of God." But it doesn't tell us exactly what that likeness is or what aspects describe what it means to be made in God's image.

Genesis 9:6 says, "Whoever sheds the blood of man, by man shall his blood be shed; for in the image of God has God made man." Though this reference is speaking of "murder" in contrast to killing as an "act of war"(which is not considered a crime), it demonstrates the sanctity of human life and the importance of being created in God's image.

1 Corinthians 11:7 states: "A man ought not to cover his head, since he is the image and glory of God." (Of course, women are created in God's image also -- Genesis 1:26, 27 -- though indirectly, as woman was created out of Adam's body. I think this verse is just emphasizing that Adam was a direct creation.)

And James 3:9 says, "With the tongue we praise our Lord and Father, and with it we curse men, who have been made in God's likeness."

Those are the references to man being made in God's image or likeness. That is all the Bible says. So how do we know what that means?

DIFFERENTIATION OF THE TERMS
"IMAGE" AND "LIKENESS"

In the Hebrew language, the word that is translated *image* in our Bibles is the word "tselem," which refers to an "image, likeness, or something cut out" -- from the root "to carve."[137] The root word of "tselem is "tsel," which means "shadow" (property or likeness).[138]

The word that is translated *likeness* is "demuth" in Hebrew. It refers to "likeness, resemblance, and similitude." "Demah" (the root of "Demuth") means "to be like or to resemble."[139] The word "demuth" is more abstract than the word "tselem."

So how have theologians distinguished the two terms? Dr. John Davis spoke in reference to the differences when he said, "These two words are best regarded as essentially synonymous."[140] Keil and Delitzsch said, "There is no possibility of discovering a sharp or well-defined difference."[141] According to McClain and Smith, they are "most likely complementary terms used to state that man is 'like God.'"[142] So, accepting the theologians' assessments, it appears that the two terms convey similar ideas.

---

[137] Francis Brown, S. R. Driver, and C. A. Briggs, Editors, *A Hebrew and English Lexicon of the Old Testament* (Oxford: Clarendon Press, 1968), 852-854.

[138] Brown, Driver, Briggs, p. 853.

[139] BDB, pp. 197-198.

[140] John J. Davis, *Paradise to Prison* (Winona Lake: BMH Books, 1975), p. 91.

[141] C. F. Keil and F. Delitzsch, "The Pentateuch," vol. 1 trans. James Martin, *Biblical Commentary on the Old Testament* (Grand Rapids: Wm. B. Eerdman's Publishing Co., 1949), p. 63.

[142] Alva J. McClain and Charles R. Smith, Unpublished syllabus of the Christian Theology class, "Salvation and Christian Life" (Grace Theological Seminary, Winona Lake, IN 1981), p. 5.

WHAT IS MEANT BY "IMAGE" OR "LIKENESS"?

A number of theologians through the years have commented on what they believe is meant by the terms *image* and *likeness*" When considering what the terms mean, Hodge stated that they are "the simple declaration of Scripture that man at his creation was like God."[143] He thought being "like God" meant, "God endowed him (man) with those attributes which belong to His own nature as a spirit . . . reason, conscience, and will. A spirit is a rational, moral, and free agent."[144]

But descriptions of the traits that God and man share are expressed by theologians in a variety of ways. McClain, Smith,[145] and Thiessen,[146] in their writings believed that "image" and "likeness" are "nonmaterial rather than physical or bodily components." Davis seemed to agree when he deemed the terms to refer to "spiritual qualities shared by God and man: self-consciousness, speech, and moral discernment (separates us from animals)."[147] McClain and Smith said that they were "personal, eternal, moral, and spiritual attributes."[148] Chafer and Walvoord thought that man was similar to God in that he was "a moral creature with intellect, capacity for feeling, and a will."[149] To Laidlaw, the terms referred to "personal, moral, and spiritual attributes" that included "intellect/rationality, self-consciousness, and personality."[150] When stating that "mental, moral, and social likeness" were part of the "image of God," Thiessen also included that man was made as a social being who seeks companionship and communion with God (Gen: 3:8).[151]

And there are more theologians "weighing in" on the discussion -- many using differing words to depict similar concepts. Ryrie expressed his

---

[143] Charles Hodge, *Systematic Theology*, vol. 2 (Grand Rapids: Wm. B. Eerdman's Publishing Co., 1979), p. 96.

[144] Charles Hodge, *Systematic Theology*, vol. 2, p. 97.

[145] McClain and Smith, "Salvation and Christian Life," p. 5

[146] H. C. Theissen, *Lectures in Systematic Theology* (Grand Rapids: Wm. B. Eerdman's Publishing Co., 1979), pp. 219-222.

[147] Davis, *Paradise to Prison*, p. 81.

[148] McClain and Smith, "Salvation & Christian Life" Syllabus, p. 5.

[149] L. S. Chafer, *Major Bible Themes*, rev. John F. Walvoord (Grand Rapids: Zondervan Publishing House, 1974), p. 167.

[150] R. A. Laidlaw, *Bible Doctrine of Man* (Edinburgh: T. and T. Clark, 1879), pp. 120-126.

[151] Theissen, *Lectures in Systematic Theology*, pp. 219-222.

idea of what the "image of God" meant this way: "The image of God in which man was created included the totality of His being as living, intelligent, determining, and moral."[152]   Erickson stated that "the image refers to the elements in the makeup of man which enable the fulfillment of his destiny. The image is the powers of personality which make man, like God, a being capable of interacting with other persons, of thinking and reflecting, and of willing freely."[153]

D. Broughton Knox was more explicit and wrote that the image of God means relationship. He wrote: "The Trinity is relationship, and humanity is relationship." God gave to us "the basic faculties and characteristics on which relationships are based." In regard to personal attributes he stated, "attributes . . . such as reflective, self-consciousness, and mind which is able to remember the past and plan for the future: . . . will, which is able to direct actions toward purpose . . . a moral sense and consciousness." Knox also talked about "a religious sense, from which we learn that we are dependent."[154]   He summarized by saying, "These characteristics, which enable humanity to be persons, have never been lost and that is why in Genesis 9 we are told we are not to raise our hand against fellow man, because he has been created in the image of God. Our fellow man is in relationship with God and with us as a person."[155]

So to summarize, theologians have said that to be in the "image" and "likeness" of God is to be a spiritual being with nonmaterial qualities who is: rational, moral, personal, self-consciousness, living, intelligent, determining, eternal, a free agent, social, relational, capable of interacting with other persons, seeking companionship and communion with God, with speech, a capacity for feeling, a will, personality, capable of thinking and reflecting, able to direct actions toward purpose and having a religious sense. We share those traits with God. And understanding that we were created with those traits helps us understand ourselves, our world, and how God wants us to relate to our world.

---

[152] Charles C. Ryrie, *Ryrie Study Bible,* (Chicago: Moody Press, 1978), p. 11.

[153] Millard J. Erickson, *Christian Theology* (Grand Rapids: Baker Book House, 1985), p. 513, paragraph 6. (This is an unabridged, one-volume edition -- originally published as three volumes: Vol. 1 (Parts 1-4), 1983; Vol. 2 (Parts 5-8), 1984; Vol. 3 (Parts 9-12), 1985.

[154] D. Broughton Knox, *The Everlasting God* (Hertfordshire: Evangelical Press, 1982), p. 66.

[155] Knox, *The Everlasting God*, p. 66.

COULD "GOD'S IMAGE" MEAN REPRESENTATIVENESS?

Dr. W. Merwin "Skip" Forbes does not agree that attributes and "functions" of man are what the Bible is talking about when it speaks of man being made in God's image. Forbes equates the concept of "image" with the idea of representation and not of certain capacities or attributes. He substantiates this concept from Ancient Near-Eastern literature where a bull would represent a god and was made in the "image" of that god. But could that bull represent that god without certain capacities or attributes? And how can we represent God if we don't know what He's like? And if we know what He's like and use that to represent Him, then aren't we picking out attributes to emulate -- just as Christ asked us to be like Him?

Forbes says that "image" equals "dominion." We are to have dominion and subdue our earth. But could dominion be a consequence or function of our being made in God's image? The position taken by this author is that the "essence" of image/likeness includes our capacities or attributes and the "function" of image/likeness refers to our representation. Seven capacities will be identified in this text: Social, Existential, Rational, Teleological, Volitional, Behavioral, and Emotional.

"God invested us with the prerequisites to fulfill our divinely appointed responsibility."[156] That we can all agree on.

TRINITY

And how does being made in God's image reflect God as it relates to the Trinity? Is God three persons in one essence or three essences in one person? The typical belief is that there are three separate, distinct persons - - Father, Son, and Holy Spirit, which is one essence -- God.

And this author believes that one God is now housed in a body. So the Father, Son, and Holy Spirit are now represented in that one body that Christ took on (Acts 7:56).

The Godhead demonstrates relationship. How does the Godhead relate to Itself? The Father loves the Son (John 3:35, 15:10). The Father sent the son (Matt. 10:40, John 16:5, 17:3, 17:18). The Son talks to the

---

[156] W. Merwin Forbes, Theological and Ethical Issues Pertaining to Life and Death (PhD diss., Grace Theological Seminary, 1982), p. 29.

Father (John 14:16, 17:1-26, etc.). The Son glorifies the Father (John 17:4). The Father sends the Spirit (John 14:16, 17). The Son sends the Spirit (John 16:7). The Spirit glorifies the Son (John 16:14).[157] How do you get all that working together?

We cannot fully understand it, yet we believe it; and somehow we were created to reflect that. We are relational – able to communicate and desire love. We desire to be loved and to have a distinct purpose that is valued and important.

"NATURE"

Another aspect to consider is a person's "nature." The Bible talks about something called man's "nature" (Col. 3:5). What is a "nature" and how does that "nature" impact man's personality?

Sometimes when we describe a person, we talk about his "nature." What is meant when that term is used?

Nature is much like personality, but it is not totally synonymous. Nature is a broader term. If you were ask "What is the nature of a tree," what wou you say?

You may respond that the nature of a tree[158] is: wood, leaves, limbs, etc. You would describe the physical realities of the tree. So "nature" includes physical entities where personality is limited to more spiritual kinds of things.

To summarize, the nature of a tree would be bark, leaves, limbs, etc., but personality would be confined to persons and refers to something immaterial. Therefore, if one were talking about the nature of an immaterial person, he would be talking about personality. If one

---

[157] Some of these relationships are cited by Loraine Boettner, Studies in Theology (Phillipsburg: The Presbyterian and Reformed Publishing co., 1974), pp. 90-91.

[158] Tree picture from http://karenswhimsy.com/tree-clipart.shtm Public Domain. Accessed 1/19/11.

were talking about the nature of a human being, it could include the body. Though the terms "nature" and "personality" are not synonymous; the term, "nature," could be used if referring to only the immaterial -- resulting in "nature" being synonymous (in that context) with "personality."

"Old Nature" vs. "New Nature"

So when theologians refer to the "old nature" and the "new nature," what are they referring to? They are NOT talking about entities. The "old nature" and "new nature" are not physical realities. The "old nature" doesn't fall off of you when you get saved. The "new nature" does not, somehow, get attached at the same time! They are not physical!

The terms "old nature" and "new nature" have been used to describe man before and after salvation -- as explained in Romans 6:6 and Colossians 3:5. The King James Version translates the terms as the "old man" and the "new man." The New American Standard uses the term "old self" in Romans 6:6 and the New International Version talks about the "earthly nature" in Colossians 3:5.

When such terms are used, they are not used to describe a material essence. The terms are metaphors. The "old man/self/nature" is simply an old set of motivations, inclinations, desires, tendencies, etc., that were part of you before you got saved. When you became a Christian, you received a "new nature," that is, a new set of motivations, inclinations, desires, tendencies, etc.

When we discuss "old nature," we are simply talking about something that was an old, earthly set. When we become saved, we have a new set, a "new nature." But we are the same metaphysical essence, BEFORE and AFTER salvation.

Before the "old man" is saved, he has one set of inclinations. He can ONLY do what is wrong. He can still do things that are helpful to others and appear to be good, but the Bible says that even our righteousness is as "filthy rags" (Isa. 64:6). No matter what good he does, it still comes out of a sin nature and CANNOT please God.

Once he accepts Christ, he is a new creature and can have a new set of inclinations and desires. He CAN now please God.

And that's why the Bible can talk about two things at the same time. The old person is "dead." Then it says, "Oh, but don't follow the old person." That seems to be a paradox. Yet, the Bible says, "Be what you already are (in Christ)."

Parents sometimes use this approach when raising their children. They may say something like, "You're a 12-year-old, so act like one!" Or they may say to their 18-year-old, "You're an adult, so act like one."

The Bible tells us we are perfected in God's eyes and so we are to act like it. We have a new nature, yet there is a war within us, where the old nature -- which does not dominate us anymore -- still lurks to lure us into temptation.

The Bible tells us the "old man" is "dead." It is not the ruler of our lives. It is not the passion of our hearts or the goal of our existence. And yet we are not to be that "old man" anymore. It is both/and. That is the great paradox of Scripture: "Be what you already are."

So we are the same metaphysical entity before and after salvation. When I got saved and I walked down to the front of the church and prayed  the prayer to accept Christ,[159] the same spirit was ALIVE, in that it was fully functioning and it was thinking, feeling, making choices, behaving, etc. My spirit was alive, but it was DEAD to the things of God. Those words: alive and dead, are metaphors.

My spirit was dead in one respect. But that doesn't mean that my metaphysical entity was slumped at the bottom of my feet and couldn't "act." No, it was alive. It was active. It was thinking. It was feeling. But it was dead to the things of God.

When I became saved, the Bible says my spirit "came alive." I did not

---

[159] Kneeling picture from *Kneeling Praying God* By: Mohamed Ibrahim from clker.com. Recolored by L. Edgington 1.8.11. clker.com is the online royalty free public domain clip art. Users who upload shared cliparts and photos on Clker.com shall certify they are in public domain, as it is shown on the upload page.

suddenly start breathing and look at myself and say, "Hey, I'm here!" No! But, NOW I could follow God and do the things of God, where before, I couldn't. It became "alive" to the things of God (metaphor).

"Natures" in Relation to the Way We Live

So how do our "natures" affect the way we live? Don't our natures fight? The Bible talks about the war within us. How do those "natures" fight?

They don't fight like some of the comics have portrayed them -- with one "nature" sitting on one shoulder and the other "nature" sitting on the other shoulder. It is not like there is a conversation going:

"Hey! You really do want to!"

"No, you don't! Don't listen to him!"

They are not entities that fight. When Scripture talks about our being "at war," it is simply saying that as human beings, we "WAR" inwardly -- Rom. 7: 23. We do battle inside of us.

"I want to make this choice, but I don't make this choice."

"I want to think that way, but I'm not thinking that way."

"I want to behave in a particular way, but I feel a pull to NOT behave that way."

So, I am at WAR, but it doesn't mean there are two entities that are doing battle in there. I do "fight" with my old nature, but there are no physical weapons or physical entities. My "fighting" simply means that sometimes I want to make bad choices and it takes strong determination to resist the temptation to make bad choices. So Christians will be characterized by their inner war!

"Old Man" vs. "New Man"

Other terms used in the Bible that characterize that "inner war" and change in "nature" are terms like "old man" and "new man."

Romans 6:6 says that the "old man" (KJV)/"old self" (NIV) was crucified with Christ. It is dead.

But, in Ephesians 4:22-24 we are told to "Put off . . . the old man (your old self) . . ." and "put on the new man" (KJV).

It says in Colossians 3:9-10, "Since you have taken off your old self ('old man' -- KJV) with its practices and have put on the new self ('new man' -- KJV)."

What does that mean -- "He's dead?" What do you mean, "put him off?" What does it mean, "You have taken off your old self?"

It is saying the same thing that we talked about in regard to natures. These are metaphors that refer to different aspects of the same immaterial essence. One aspect needs to be resisted as we choose to serve God. It is talking about that one immaterial essence that "wars" within us.

Again, when it says that the "old man" was "crucified," it means that the person who ONLY had the capability of sinning -- of moving away from God -- is now dead. I have a new life in that I have a capacity now to please God. I didn't have that before. As a "new man," as a new person, I can please God.

But in this life, I will continually be at "war" and need to be on constant guard with perseverance to "put off" the "old man" and "put on" the "new self" -- to be the person that God intends for me to be. I am no longer characterized by the "old man," but I still do battle with the old nature.

Conclusion

We have spent all of this time in order to try to understand "person" and to begin to look at the idea of "personality." In order to have personality and be a person, we have to be spirit beings. The spirit being is made in the image and likeness of God. With our personality -- which is an outworking of our spiritual "likeness" of God, we are going to be able to do some things that God wants us to do and that is: to represent Him. We have the divine prerequisites (essence of image of God) to carry out our responsibility: to represent God (function of image of God).

And yes, each of us has a personality, even though we might say, "Well, she really doesn't have a personality," or "You know, he could really use a personality." In reality, those statements are not accurate. She may not be very flamboyant. He may not be doing much to demonstrate what is inside of him. But each still has a personality -- a full-fledged, functioning personality.

Though not discussed in detail in this book, this author distinguishes seven capacities (Social, Existential, Rational, Teleological, Volitional, Emotional, and Behavioral)[160] to explain the various aspects that comprise the "essence" of one's "person" or "personality" -- the image of God. The God-like capacities enable us to carry out our divinely appointed function and make up a theory of personality that is used by this author as a model for counseling.

In the following chapter we will look at an aspect of imperfect man's personhood or "psyche" – especially after sin entered. We will be looking at the unconscious especially as it pertains to sin.

Freud believed that a major part of one's personality had to do with unconscious forces; therefore, in his theory are major determinants in the development of one's personality. Is there a realm in our minds that is unconscious? Does the Bible refer to such a realm? The next chapter explores these questions.

---

[160] Thomas J. Edgington, *Theological Foundations of Counseling* (Winona Lake, IN: Edgington Publications, 2013). Printed by Lulu.com.

CHAPTER 5

SENSATION AND PERCEPTION

When God created us, he invested within us the necessary capabilities to perceive the world around us (Prov. 20:12; Ps. 94:9). He gave us five senses: seeing, hearing, smelling, tasting, and touching (God has these as well – Ps. 115:3-8). With these senses, we "sense" our world, and then with our rational capacity, we attempt to "make sense" of it. In most Introduction to Psychology courses, sensation and perception are aspects of the class. Myers defines sensation as "the process by which our sensory receptors and nervous system receive and represent stimulus energies from our environment."[161] He then defines perception as "the process of organizing and interpreting sensory information, enabling us to recognize meaningful object and events."[162] Because God created us with these capabilities, it only makes sense that these would be addressed in Scripture.

In regard to sight, sometimes the Bible refers to actual sight (Deut. 34:7, Rev. 1:7) and to metaphorical "sight" (Matt. 6:22, 23; 7:3-5; 13:16; Rev. 3:18). Metaphorically speaking some can see with their eyes but cannot "see" with their heart (John 3:3). The Word is certainly necessary to have the sight necessary to see our way (Ps. 119:105).

Part of Jesus' ministry was bringing sight to the blind (Mark 8:22-24; 10:46-52; John 9:2-3). The story in Mark 8:22-24 is especially interesting because Jesus spit on the man's eyes which brought partial healing, and then put his hands on the man's eyes and his sight was completely restored. In John 9:2-7, Jesus spit on the ground and made mud with his saliva and put it on the man's eyes. The man then washed in a pool and received back his sight. It makes one wonder why Jesus chose these methods or why one had only partial results and then full. Certainly each man felt the sensation of spit and mud before seeing again!

When God called Paul (who was Saul at the time), he caused Saul to become blind until Ananias placed his hands on Saul. Something like

---

[161] David G. Myers, *Exploring Psychology, 9th Ed.* (New York: Worth Publishers, 2014)   p. 192.

[162] Myers, *Exploring Psychology, 9th Ed.,* p. 192

scales fell from Saul's eyes and his sight was restored (Acts 9:8-18). God may have wanted Saul to understand how "blind" he was without God, and He may have wanted Saul to be utterly dependent on others for a time. Whatever His motive, God got Saul's attention!

While sight is something very important, the Bible makes it clear that we live by faith and not sight (2 Cor. 5:7). Heb. 11:1 tells us that "faith is being sure of what we hope for and certain of what we do not see." Faith is the true "sight" that God wants us to have.

In regard to the sense of smell, the Bible refers to fragrance and pleasing aromas in a literal sense (Ex. 30:38; Ps. 45:8; John 12:3) and pleasing aromas to God, which most likely refers to Him being pleased with the offering rather than a literal sense of smell (Gen. 8:21; Lev. 8:21; Lev. 26:31; Ps. 141:2; Phil. 4:18). It also refers to stench as opposed to fragrance (Isa. 3:24).

In the more figurative sense, the Bible states that we, as Christians, are the aroma of Christ among those in the world (2 Cor. 2:15). Aroma is often used to attract (perfume and cologne are prime examples!), and our lives should be such that we are attracting others to Christ. Not only should we smell good, we should taste good too! (Matt. 5:13).

When referring to taste, the Bible says that we are to be the salt of the earth (Matt. 5:13) and that our conversations are to be "seasoned with salt" (Col. 4:6) displaying the grace of God. The Bible, as with the other senses mentioned so far, refers to taste in a metaphorical way (Ps. 119:103; Matt. 16:28; Heb. 2:9) and in a literal way (Prov. 24:13; Col. 2:21). Metaphorically speaking, we are to "taste and see" that the Lord is good (Ps. 34:8) as we take refuge in Him.

The sense of touch seemed to be an important one in Jesus's ministry. Touch was involved in his healing (Matt. 9:21, 29-30, Mark 5:41) and in his care for children (Mark 10:13-16). He seems to be showing us that touch is a crucial part of loving others, especially children. Paul tells us that this is very important in marriage (1 Cor. 7:1-5).

Our five senses are a crucial part of the scientific method. We gather data through our five senses, and then attempt to make sense of it. Harold Faw states, "We give special status to information that has been verified and confirmed by our senses, calling such information scientific."[163] John tells us that we proclaim Christ because we know he is real. Why? Because the disciples had heard, seen, and touched Him (1 John 1:1-4). When Christ appeared to his disciples after He rose from the grave, He told them to "touch me and see" for evidence that it was Jesus and not a ghost (Luke 24:39). He used their senses to increase their faith. Science is an important tool for studying the created domain, and our senses are an integral part of that. In the end, all will bow down and confess Christ because they will experience Him (Isa. 45:23; Rom. 14:11; Phil. 2:10). Their senses will tell them that He is Lord, and that everything He said was true!

Perception, as stated earlier, is "the process of organizing and interpreting sensory information."[164] When we are engaged in the work of science, we can do a good job of using our senses to gather data, but that does not ensure that our findings are accurate. We can interpret good data in wrong ways. The Bible refers to those who have faulty worldviews and faulty interpretations because they cannot "see" truth (Matt. 6:23-24, John 3:3; Titus 1:15). Unless Christ draws us to Himself (John 6:44) and enlightens "the eyes of the heart" (Eph. 1:18), we will not correctly interpret the data we find. Jesus is the light of the world (John 8:12) and without him, we walk in darkness. God tells us to call to Him, and that He will "tell you great and unsearchable things you do not know" (Jer. 33:3). His thoughts are higher than ours and His ways are superior to ours (Isa. 55:8-9); therefore if we want a proper sense of perception, we better stay close to Him and His Word.

This is why asking for discernment is such an important part of our prayer lives (Phil. 1:9-10). As we follow God, study His Word, and grow in maturity, we can be trained to distinguish good from evil (Heb. 5:14). One area that needs special discernment is the topic of ESP, or extra sensory perception. How should the Christian view this realm that goes beyond ordinary perceptual experiences? Is it of God? Satan? Or simply human?

Extrasensory perception (ESP) is part of a discipline known as parapsychology. ESP includes telepathy, clairvoyance and precognition. Telepathy is "mind to mind communication – one person sending thoughts

---

[163] Harold W. Faw, *Psychology in Christian Perspective* (Grand Rapids, MI: Baker Books, 1995) p. 49.

[164] Myers, *Exploring Psychology, 9th Ed.*, p. 192.

to another or perceiving another's thoughts."[165] Clairvoyance involves "perceiving remote events, such as sensing that a friend's house is on fire."[166] Precognition is "perceiving future events, such as a political leader's death or a sporting event's outcome."[167] Psychokinesis, which involves moving objects with one's mind is considered a part of parapsychology, but does not fall under the heading of ESP.

As we discussed in Chapter 3, we are spirit beings who are housed in bodies and our spirits are capable of engaging in all of the psychological functions (thinking, choosing, emotions) that happen in the body (Luke 16:19-31). If this is the case, could spirits "communicate" with one another without bodily activity? Don't we communicate to God this way at times? Can the Holy Spirit help us sense things that are beyond the physical sphere? Many Christians tell stories of such occurrences. Prophets foretold the future in the Old Testament. Are there those with such powers today? Many sincere Christians believe so.

The Bible uses the word "divination" to speak of the attempt to obtain "secret or hidden knowledge" from the spirit world. In fact, in Deuteronomy 18:9-11, God strictly prohibits such activity. Some might say that this passage only applies to the occult in which someone is seeking information from demonic sources. Faw states "Although there is debate as to whether ESP is necessarily associated with the occult, these warnings indicate that great caution and discernment are needed in dealing with the issues."[168] In Deuteronomy 29:29, Moses wrote, "The secret things belong to the Lord our God, but the things revealed belong to us and to our sons forever, that we may observe all the words of this law." Our primary concern should be what is revealed in God's Word rather than some secret or hidden knowledge.

Can science add anything to what Scripture teaches? James Randi, a magician and skeptic of ESP, has a longstanding offer (now $1 million) "to anyone who proves a genuine psychic powers under proper observing conditions."[169] Not one person has emerged. "Randi's offer has been

---

[165] David G. Myers, *Exploring Psychology*, 7th Ed. (New York: Worth Publishers, 2008)   p. 176.

[166] Myers, *Exploring Psychology*, 7th Ed, p. 176.

[167] Myers, *Exploring Psychology*, 7th Ed., p. 176.

[168] Faw, *Psychology in Christian Perspective*, p. 46.

[169] J. Randi, *Two Thousand Club Mailing List Email Letter* (1999).

publicized for three decades and dozens of people have been tested, sometimes under the scrutiny of an independent panel of judges. Still, nothing."[170]

Maybe there are times that God breaks in and does the extraordinary and maybe the Holy Spirit gives special insight to some at certain times. We ought to remain open – because God can do whatever He wants to – and He certainly has the power to do so. But maybe some of these things that seem to come from a special power may be trickery, coincidence, or illusory correlations. It could just be us wishing something to be true.

So what is a good position for the Christian to hold? I would say: Be open. Be very cautious. Don't be afraid to gather data to confirm or disconfirm. And focus on what is clearly revealed – God's Word.

---

[170] Myers, *Exploring Psychology, 7th Ed.*, p. 178.

CHAPTER 6

LEVELS OF CONSCIOUSNESS

In Freud's original theory of personality, he divided consciousness into three levels: the conscious, the preconscious, and the unconscious. The conscious "includes all of the sensations and experiences of which we are aware at any given moment."[171] The preconscious is "the storehouse of memories, perceptions, and thoughts of which we are not consciously aware at the moment but we can easily summon into consciousness."[172] The preconscious can be triggered with a stimulus. If you were asked to think about your favorite pet (assuming you had a pet), a memory would come to mind. You were not consciously thinking about that pet until the question triggered your memory.

Freud believed that the conscious and preconscious levels were only the tip of the iceberg. The larger portion, the unconscious, is below the surface. For Freud, our deepest wishes and desires are part of this realm. For Freud, the unconscious contains the major driving power behind all behaviors and is the repository of forces we cannot see or control."[173] What does the Bible have to say about these levels of consciousness?

The Bible refers to the conscious realm (Rom. 3:20, 1 Peter 2:19). Our experience certainly confirms its presence – you could not be reading this right now if you were not conscious! The Bible, while not calling it our "preconscious," does refer to memory (Prov. 10:7; Matt. 26:13; 1 Thes. 3:6). Again, this fits our experience. But what about the unconscious?

As a psychologist who is aware of how the unconscious is a major part of the history of psychology, this author has always been intrigued with this topic. Interest was especially piqued when I was working with victims of abuse who suddenly (in my office!) had memories of abuse that they had "forgotten." (Before that, they did not even know they had been

---

[171] D. P. Schultz & S. E. Schultz, *Theories of Personality* (Belmont, CA: Wadsworth/Cengage Learning, 2013) p. 48.

[172] Schultz & Schultz, *Theories of Personality*, p. 45.

[173] Schultz & Schultz, *Theories of Personality*, p. 49.

abused!) Where did these memories go? Did these memories have an effect on their behavior even though there was no awareness of these events?

Logic alone tells us that an unconscious aspect of ourselves exists. As we examine the Johari window (named after Joe Luft and Harry Ingram),[174] we find a four-celled personality paradigm.

	Known to Self	Unknown to Self
Known to Others	Public	Blind
Unknown to Others	Secret	Unconscious

Things that are known to self and known to others are considered public knowledge. That which is unknown to self yet known to others would fall in the "blind" category. The Bible speaks of "blindness" metaphorically as the dulling of the intellect (John 12:40; 2 Cor. 4:4; 1 John 2:11).[175] A good example is the person who can see a splinter in another's eye, yet is unable to see the log in his own   (Matt. 7:1-6).

Things that are known to the self but unknown to others are considered "secret." The Bible considers those who "conceal themselves" (root 'alam)[176] as deceitful men and hypocrites (Ps. 26:4). God discovers all things because He knows the secrets ("hidden things") of the heart (Ps. 44:21). And God is aware of our secret iniquities or hidden sins as well (Ps. 90:8). "The holy light of God illuminates the hidden corners of the

---

[174] I.D. Yalom, *The Theory and Practice of Group Psychotherapy* (New York: Basic Books, 1985), p. 493.

[175] W.E. Vine, *A Comprehensive Dictionary of the Original Greek Words with their Precise Meanings for English Readers* (McLean: MCDonald, 1940), p. 136.

[176] Francis Brown, S.R. Driver, and C.A. Briggs, *A Hebrew and English Lexicon of the Old Testament* (Oxvord: Claridon Press, 1968), p. 761.

heart and exposes its dark secrets."[177]   The New Testament also refers to that which is secret, hidden, or concealed   (Rom. 2:16; 1 Cor. 14:25).

The realm of the "unconscious" is that which is unknown to self and unknown to others.   Certainly logic points to such a realm, and it only follows that if "secret sins" exist (Ps. 90:8), then unconscious sins may exist as well.

In order to understand the nature of unconscious sin as taught in the Bible, it is vital to understand the attributes of and differences between the purification/sin (hatta't) offering of   Lev. 4:1-5:13 and the reparation/guilt ('asam) offering of Lev. 5:14-6:7.

There are two kinds of purification offerings in Lev. 4:1-5:13. The first involves purification offerings for inadvertent sins (4:1-35). The second involves the purification offering for sins of omission (5:1-13).[178]

Inadvertent sin is obviously different from deliberate sin.   This is shown in Numbers 15:27ff, which "contrasts unwitting sin with sinning 'with a high hand' (v.30), i.e. blatantly or deliberately.   The sinner who sins 'with a high hand' will not be forgiven, but cut off, whereas one who sins inadvertently can offer a sacrifice and enjoy forgiveness."[179]

According to Wenham, "purification is the main element in the purification sacrifice.   Sin not only angers God and deprives Him of His due, it also makes His sanctuary unclean.   A holy God cannot dwell amid uncleanness."[180]   Restitution is the key idea for the reparation offering, and propitiation of divine anger is the important element for the burnt offering (Lev. 1:1-17).

In Lev. 4:1-35, we find the discussion of purification offerings for sins committed inadvertently (bisegaga).   According to Milgrom, "inadvertent wrongdoing may result from two causes: negligence or ignorance.   Either the offender knows the law but involuntarily violates it or he acts knowingly but is unaware he did wrong.   The former situation underlies the examples   of   accidental   homicide   (Numbers   35:16-18,   22-23;

[177] The NIV Study Bible (Grand Rapids: Zondervan Bible Publishers, 1985), p. 883.

[178] G. J. Wenham, The Book of Leviticus in the New International Commentary on the Old Testament (Grand Rapids: Wm. B. Eerdmans, 1979), p. 165.

[179] Wenham, The Book of Leviticus, p. 92.

[180] Wenham, The book of Leviticus in the New International Commentary on the Old Testament,   p. 87.

Deuteronomy 19:5-6) and the latter is preserved by 1 Samuel 14:32-34; Ezekiel 45:20, and such nonritual texts as 1 Samuel 26:21; Proverbs 5:23; Job 6:24; 19:4."[181]

Milgrom goes on to say that "these two types of inadvertence have also been termed 'error' and 'accident.' In either case, as the citations illustrate, unconsciousness of the sin and consciousness of the act are always presumed."[182]

If a sin is inadvertent or unconscious, how does it become known? According to Wenham,

> the situation here envisaged seems to be as follows: the 'congregation' representing all Israel goes astray, but the fault is hidden from the assembly, that is, it is not brought to light in the course of worship in the assembly in the daily services. How this could have come about is obscure. Perhaps a vision or prophecy or operation of the Urim and Thummim is intended. At any rate, the fault does not appear to affect the conduct of worship. But the congregation starts to feel guilty (v.13), and then the sin by which they have incurred guilt becomes known. Then the assembly brings the bull as an offering and the sanctuary is cleaned.[183]

An example could be a situation in which a high priest declares a new moon on the wrong day. Everyone is conscious of the act, but not conscious of the sin.

In the Old Testament, the purification made possible the continuing presence of God among His people. The place of worship was cleaned, so that God could remain. In the New Testament, the worshipper (as opposed to the place of worship) needs to be cleaned, and the avenue of purification is accepting Christ as the One who brings remission of sins.

---

[181] Jacob Milgrom, *Leviticus 1-16, A New Translation with Instruction and Commentary. The Anchor Bible* (New York: Doubleday, 1967), p. 228.

[182] Milgrom, *Leviticus 1-16* , p. 228.

[183] Wendham, *The Book of Leviticus*, pp. 98-99.

"As with the other sacrifices in Leviticus, the coming of Christ has made the purification offering obsolete."[184]

In Leviticus 5:1-4 we find the second category of sins requiring atonement by means of a purification offering. "The common factor in these sins is that someone knows he ought to do something, but then forgets about it; it slips his memory (vv. 2,3,4)."[185]

What can we learn from the Old Testament laws? "These   Old Testament laws show that unintentional sin is just as much sin in God's sight as deliberate wrongdoing."[186]

However, the solutions for different sins vary. According to Milgrom, "confession is never required for inadvertence, but only for deliberate sins. Indeed, there are only four passages in P in which confession (hitwadda) is explicitly required, and each case deals exclusively with deliberate sin (5:1-4; 16:21; 26:40, Numbers 5:6-7)."[187]

He further states:

> for involuntary sin, 'asam or remorse alone suffices: it renders confession superfluous. For deliberate sin, however, confession is demanded over and above remorse. But what function does confession serve? Why must contrition of the heart be augmented by the confirmation of the lips? Confession must, then, play a vital role in the judicial process. Because it only occurs when deliberate sin is expiated by sacrifice, the conclusion is ineluctable: confession is the legal device fashioned by the Priestly legislators to convert deliberate sins into inadvertence, thereby qualifying them for sacrificial expiation. Confession, then, is a sine qua non in Hittite religion for attaining divine forgiveness."[188]

This is also true in the New Testament. "Confession of sin is a prerequisite of cleansing (1 John 1:9). For a Christian, the animal offering

---

184 Wendham, *The Book of Leviticus*, p. 102.

185 Wendham, *The Book of Leviticus*, p. 93.

186 Wendham, *The Book of Leviticus*, p. 103.

187 Milgrom, *Leviticus 1-16*, p. 301.

188 Milgrom, *Leviticus 1-16*, pp. 301-302.

is no longer necessary, since Christ's death has brought purification, but confession is, if fellowship with God is to be reestablished."[189]

The reparation offering of Leviticus 5:14-6:7 is different from the purification offering, in that the latter brought purification, whereas the former brought restitution and compensation. With the reparation offering, damage has been done, and restitution is needed.

In Leviticus 5 and 6, reparation offering is ordered for inadvertent sin (5:14-19) and for deliberate sin (6:1-7). In Leviticus 5:14-19, two kinds of inadvertent sin are cited. The first (5:14-16) is similar to that mentioned in Leviticus 4:1-35 pertaining to the purification offering. The second (5:17-19) is especially important to the discussion of unconscious sin.

The reparation offering appears to involve sinning inadvertently against the Lord's sacred property. "The word translated 'sacred property' is literally 'holy things.'"[190] This offering "demonstrates that there is an aspect of sin not covered by the other sacrifices. It is that of satisfaction or compensation."[191]

The term translated "inadvertence" (bisegaga), in Leviticus 5:14-16, "implies the existence of consciousness,"[192] that is consciousness of the act but unconsciousness of the sin. As stated earlier, "either the offender knows the laws but involuntarily violates it or he acts knowingly but is unaware he did wrong."[193] The sin is due to negligence or ignorance regarding sacred property or holy things. An example might be someone who inadvertently ate holy food. The person was commanded to compensate for the loss, along with adding some to it (Leviticus 22:2-14).

In Leviticus 5:17-19,

the term segaga, normally rendered 'inadvertence,' implies consciousness, that is to say, awareness of the act. For this reason it is missing in the protasis, the statement of the case

---

[189] Wendham, *The Book of Leviticus*, p. 103.

[190] Wendham, *The Book of Leviticus*, p. 106.

[191] Wendham, *The Book of Leviticus*, p. 111.

[192] Milgrom, *Leviticus 1-16*, p. 228.

[193] Milgrom, *Leviticus 1-16*, p. 228.

(v.17), which explicitly declares that it was an unconscious act, welo yada 'without knowing it.' How then are we to account for its appearance here in the apodosis? The answer, I believe, is that it is the object of the verb kipper 'expiate.' There needs to be a term denoting an unconscious wrong that will be expiated by the reparation offering; but there is not such term in the Priestly vocabulary. This is all the more surprising because there is a plethora of words to describe deliberate sins (16:16; Numbers 15:30-31). Yet the regrettable fact is that P has only one term to describe as inadvertent sin, segaga, but of a specific kind, a consciously committed inadvertence. Other scriptural sources are not so impaired, for example nisharot 'unperceived errors' (Ps. 19:13); ta'alumot 'hidden things' (Job 11:16). This P must resort to periphrasis, literature, 'his inadvertencies that he committed though he did not know,' in order words, segaga is expanded to mean an accidental wrong followed by the qualification that it was committed (un?) consciously. To be sure, a more unambiguous circumlocution would have been chosen, such as "aser hata' wehu' lo' yada' 'that which he sinned without knowing it.

It appears, however, that the framers of this law wanted to stress the organic unity of the two cases that comprise the topic of sacrilege against sanita: both are inadvertencies (segaga), but whereas the first is committed consciously (vv.14-16), the second is committed unconsciously, we (hu') lo' yada' (vv. 17-19).[194]

Thus in Leviticus 5:17-19, we find one of the most feared sins in antiquity -- one in which there is both unconsciousness of the act and its sinfulness. No wonder it was dreaded by the ancients! How does one discover such a sin? According to Wenham, "the discovery that he has done wrong comes through his conscience. He feels guilty and starts to suffer for it, i.e., bears his iniquity."[195] After suspecting sin, he fears the worst and brings a reparation offering. "This sacrifice served then to pacify oversensitive Israelites' consciences."[196]

---

[194] Milgrom, *Leviticus 1-16*, p. 334.

[195] Wendham, *The Book of Leviticus*, pp. 107-108.

[196] Wendham, *The Book of Leviticus*, p. 108.

According to Milgrom, "concern over unconscious sin also permeates the Bible (e.g., Deuteronomy 29:28; 1 Samuel 26:19; Psalm 19:13; Job 1:5). Indeed, a case can be made that Job's polemic against his friends rest on their disagreement over the role of traditional view of Israel and its environment that Job is suffering for his unconscious sin; Job, by contrast, empathetically denies this doctrine and insists that his suffering is unjustified until he knows wherein he has sinned."[197]

God, of course, never answers Job and his friends regarding the question, "Are we accountable and punished for unconscious sin?" He teaches Job that suffering may be in instrument of God for good (causing growth in our lives) and not a punishment for sin.

Leviticus 6:1-7 is the passage in which the reparation offering is ordered for deliberate sins. How can this be, since deliberate sin is not to be forgiven, and the sinner cut off from the assembly (Numbers 15:27ff)? "It seems likely that atonement for deliberate sins was possible where there was evidence of true repentance, demonstrated by remorse (feeling guilty), full restitution, and confession of sin."[198] According to Milgrom, "the repentance of the sinner through remorse and confession reduces the intentional sin to an inadvertence, thereby rendering it eligible for sacrificial expiation."[199]

To close the discussion regarding offerings, it should be remembered that the burnt offering brought reconciliation, the purification offering brought purification, and the reparation offering brought satisfaction or compensation through payment for the sin. Praise God--this was all performed by Jesus Christ once for all!

In returning to the discussion regarding unconscious sin, it is vital to analyze a passage previously mentioned: Psalm 19:12-13. Three categories of wrongdoing are listed in these verses: two of which are accidental and the other deliberate. The psalmist declares "Who can discern segi'ot, clear me from nistarot, restrain your servant from zedim.

In his article regarding the cultic segagah, Milgrom states, "On logic alone we could deduce that if the latter category of nistarot concerns acts of which the doer is unconscious and which are sinful, the former, the

---

[197] Milgrom, *Leviticus 1-16,* p. 362.

[198] Wendham, *The Book of Leviticus*, p. 109.

[199] Milgrom, *Leviticus 1-16*, p. 373.

segi'ot must refer to acts of which the doer is conscious but whose sinfulness he learns afterwards."[200] According to Milgrom, these two types of accidental sin are set off as against the zedim, the deliberate sins of Psalm 19:13a.

Milgrom goes on to say, "The verbs employed with each category corroborate their specialized meaning. 'Discern' implies the conviction of the misdemeanor with knowledge; (the root bin, in any of its aspects, never connotes consciousness!) The psalmist has extolled the keeping of the Law for its manifold benefits (vs. 8-12) but he now asks the rhetorical question: Who can know the entire law and thereby prevent inadvertencies? *Furthermore, beyond the scope of law and human wisdom lies the unchartable realm of the hidden, the unconscious sins* (emphasis added). In this matter, he can only turn to God and implore that he be cleared. Finally, as regards deliberate sins, man requires restraint in the face of temptation and passion and for this he asks divine aid. Having covered the entire range of human evil, the psalmist's conclusion follows irrefutably: 'then I shall be perfect.'"[201]

It is evident that the Bible teaches the existence of unconscious sins. This follows what the prophet asks in Jeremiah 17:9, "The heart is deceitful above all things and beyond cure. Who can understand it?" and the psalmist who asks, "If you, O Lord, kept a record of sins, O Lord, who could stand?" (Psalm 130:3).

It only follows, then, that people could engage in "good" behavior (even 'biblical' behavior) yet from evil motives, and not even realize it. The Bible teaches that motives are important to God (1 Chronicles 28:9; 1 Corinthians 4:5) and that some people look "good" on the outside, but will not fool God who sees the heart (1 Samuel 16:7; Matthew 7:21-23; Luke 11:37-54; Luke 18:9-14; 18-30; Philippians 1:15-18; Revelation 3:14-22).

This is why it is crucial for those in the field of psychology and the helping profession to understand unconscious sins, motives, and the depth of the human heart (Proverbs 20:5). Otherwise, we may be blinded by "biblical" behavior that in reality is far from biblical! External behavior is important to God, but so is the internal reality emitting the behavior (Psalm 51:16-19; Matthew 15:16-20).

Both the Bible and our logic point to the existence of three levels of consciousness. One level is the unconscious, and the Bible teaches the

---

[200] Milgrom, *Leviticus 1-16*, p. 120.

[201] Milgrom, *Leviticus 1-16 . . .* , p. 181.

184

notion that sin is a part of this realm. Another question emerges: "What else could be a part of this realm?" Freud believed that dreams were a part of the unconscious – in fact, he said it was "the royal road to the unconscious."[202] The next chapter will focus on states of unconsciousness, including dreams. Meditation and hypnosis will also be discussed.

---

[202] Freud, *The Interpretation of Dreams*, p. 680.

CHAPTER 7
STATES OF CONSCIOUSNESS

Dreams

Without fail, every time I teach a psychology course that contains dreams as one of the topics, students show more excitement, engage in more discussion, and tell more of their own stories than any other topic. I would guess that all of us share similar feelings. There is something very intriguing about dreams.

I am going to make an assumption that God created us with an ability to dream. Otherwise, we would have to conclude that dreams are a result of the fall and, therefore, something sinful. If God wanted us to dream, it only makes sense to ask the question, "What is the purpose of dreams?"

There are many theories about why we dream. Freud thought that "the dream is the disguised fulfillment of a repressed wish."[203] Those wishes are converted bodily desires such as food, water, and sex. The activation synthesis model suggests that as certain areas of the brain are activated at night, dreams are the subjective interpretation of that brain activity.[204] Others say that the brain is cleaning up the clutter of the mind to get us prepared for the next day.[205] Another says it is actually a form of psychotherapy, helping us deal with our issues in a safe environment.[206] Still others claim that dreams have some sort of adaptive function, either physiologically or psychologically. One psychological function could be that of problem-solving.[207]

What does the Bible say about the function of dreams? I believe the

---

[203] A. A. Brill - Editor, *The Basic Writings of Sigmund Freud* (New York: The Modern Library, 1938), p. 235.

[204] J. A. Hobson, *Sleep* (New York: Scientific American Library, 1995).

[205] C. Evans & E. Newman, "Dreaming: An Analogy from Computers," *New Scientist*, (419,577-579), 1964.

[206] E. Hartmann, "Making Connections in s Safe Place: Is Dreaming Psychotherapy?" *Dreaming*, 5, 213-228 (1995).

[207] G. W. Domhoff, *The Case for a Cognitive Theory of Dreams*, (2010), Retrieved September 21, 2013 from the World Wide Web: Http//dreamresearch.net/Library/domhoff_2010.htm.

Bible gives at least four purposes, but this list is by no means exhaustive. Dreams were sometimes used by God as a means of revelation. In 1 Kings 3:5, the Lord appeared to Solomon in a dream and told him to "ask for whatever you want me to give to you." He appeared to Joseph and the wise men (Matt. 1:20-21, 2:12-23) to tell them what they should do. It begs the question: "Does God reveal things to us in dreams today?" We have the Bible as His written revelation, but could he reveal personal information to us like He did to Joseph and the wise men?

I know of someone who said he had a very clear dream in which God appeared to him and said that he should not let his wife have an upcoming surgery for her cancer. In the dream, God said, "I will heal her without any medical intervention, to show my power." Was this revelation from God? What should he have done? What would you do?

Another function of dreams found in Scripture appears to be that of giving us warnings. In Job 33:14-18, it states that "in a dream, in a vision of the night, He (God) may speak in their ears and terrify them with warning to turn man from wrongdoing." Could dreams have this adaptive function? One researcher believes so. McNamara suggests "that nightmares are like other adaptive system.[208] He goes on to say that "nightmares can be compared to a fever: unpleasant, but adaptive and even life-giving."[209] McNamara believed that nightmares can be a sign that the person having this "compelling and memorable emotional experience"[210] is "in danger of experiencing a major misfortune."[211] This sign could lead the person to consult with others or seek help which in turn could lead to a better outcome. He goes on to say, "with a little help from an experienced professional who affirms and supports the individual's sense of self, dreams and even nightmares can once again be experienced as sources of renewal, hope, and change."[212] Could God use dreams with

---

[208] Patrick McNamara, *Nightmares: The Science and Solution of Those Frightening Visions During Sleep* (Praeger Publishers, 2008), p. 148.

[209] McNamara, *Nightmares: The Science and Solution of Those Frightening Visions During Sleep*, p. 148.

[210] McNamara, *Nightmares: The Science and Solution of Those Frightening Visions During Sleep*, p. 149.

[211] McNamara, *Nightmares: The Science and Solution of Those Frightening Visions During Sleep*, p. 149.

[212] McNamara, *Nightmares: The Science and Solution of Those Frightening Visions During Sleep*, p. 150.

this positive adaptive function?

In Ecclesiastes 5:3, it begins with, "As a dream comes when there are many cares . . . ." Do dreams tell us something about our worries, fears, and concerns? Domhoff believes they do. While refuting the idea that dreams offer solutions to one's problems, he does say that dreams surely reflect problems.[213] He states, "Because dreams often seem to draw upon the same conceptions and concerns that are central to a person's waking life, they do have psychological meaning and they therefore can portray central emotional preoccupations in creation and dramatic ways."[214]

When I was in college, I would often dream that I was in a semester in which I had five classes, but I was only showing up to four of them. Half-way through the semester, I would realize that I had not attended one of my classes and I'd then race to where the class was meeting. Of course, the whole class (including the professor) was there when I arrived and the dream ended. When I started teaching college classes, I would dream a similar dream in which I was not showing up to one of the classes I was teaching! This probably says something about my fears of not being responsible and therefore, "getting into trouble." Recurring dreams probably have some kind of psychological meaning – and often they have to do with our worries and concerns.

The last function of dreams may give some credence to Freud's theory of dreaming, although his theory, as a whole, does not find scriptural support (or even support from the psychological research community). He believed that dreams are "disguised fulfillments of repressed wishes"[215] or what we call "wish fulfillment."

Isaiah 29:7-8 says, "As it is with a dream, with a vision in the night – as when hungry people dream, they are eating, but they awaken, and their hunger remains: as when thirsty people dream they are drinking, but they awaken faint, with their thirst unquenched." Dreams may be our mind's way of trying to meet our needs – this passage refers to our physical needs. Could this also be true for our psychological needs – deep longings for loving relationships and meaningful impact in our world?

The Bible seems to indicate that dreams have a purpose and are sometimes used by God. In counseling, if a client strongly wishes to

[213] Domhoff, *The Case for a Cognitive Theory of Dreams*, p. 10.

[214] Domhoff, *The Case for a Cognitive Theory of Dreams*, p. 4.

[215] Sigmund Freud, *The Interpretation of Dreams* (Germany: Franz Deuticke,1900), p. 608

discuss a dream (especially recurrent dreams), I may use them to reinforce what we have been discussing in our sessions. Dreams can give powerful images to their psychological problems, and can be helpful if used for godly purposes. But the Bible gives a strong warning to us when it says, "Much dreaming and many words are meaningless" (Ecc. 5:7). If we place too much emphasis on interpreting dreams, we may miss what is central to helping our clients. God's Word is our authority and dependence on the Holy Spirit is necessary. But could the Spirit sometimes use dreams to guide us and help us? Good question!

Meditation

Meditation is another aspect of consciousness. In fact, some believe it is a way of achieving a "higher" state of consciousness. This is the case with Transcendental Meditation or TM. TM is a form of mantra mediation introduced in India in 1955. Through relaxation, the mind transcends all mental activity so that consciousness is open to itself. The goal is to lower stress and enhance the individual's creative potential, thus leading to success in everyday life.

Some Christians have turned to various forms of Eastern meditation to alleviate stress, relax, and achieve a higher state of "spirituality." In the past few years, yoga has become increasingly popular among Christians. Is there any harm in this?

According to Groothuis (2004), "Yoga, deeply rooted in Hinduism, essentially means to be "yoked" with the divine. Yogic postures, breathing, and chanting were originally designed not to bring better physical health and well-being (Western marketing to the contrary), but a sense of oneness with Brahman – the Hindu word for the absolute being that pervades all things.[216]

Both TM and Yoga attempt to achieve a higher state of consciousness, to receive new experiences, or a form of "enlightenment." The question is: "Is that a goal of the Christian?" Two questions that follow: "What does the Bible say about meditation?" and "What does it say about achieving a higher state of consciousness?"

---

[216] Douglas Groothuis, *Dangerous Meditation*, (Christianity Today, 2004), para. 3. Retrieved from http://www.christianitytoday.com/ct/2004/november/10.78.html

There are many passages in the Bible that refers to meditation. Joshua 1:8 tells us to "meditate on it [the Book of the Law] day and night." Psalm 19:14 says "May the words of my mouth and the meditation of my heart be pleasing in your sight." Psalm 48:9 states, "Within your temple, O God, we meditate on your unfailing love." Psalm 77:12 says, "I will meditate on all your works and consider all of your mighty deeds." Psalm 104:34 states, "May my meditation be pleasing to him, as I rejoice in the Lord." Psalm 119:15 says, "I meditate on your precepts and consider your ways." Psalm 119:148 states, "My eyes stay open through the watches of the night – that I may meditate on your promises."

These verses are not referring to achieving a "higher form of consciousness" or clearing out minds to receive new experiences. There are clear objects with biblical meditation: we are to meditate on God's Word, His unfailing love, His works and mighty deeds, His precepts, and His promises. The goal is not receiving new revelation or insights, rather to strongly concentrate on the revelation He has already given us, so that we can use that revelation for His glory and for His work.

Paul, in writing to the Colossians, warned against a particular heresy ("Gnosticism") that advocated a "secret knowledge" or a type of asceticism that would help people transcend evil and the corruption of the world. This special knowledge was superior to faith and would lead to a type of "salvation" for its followers. The goal was to look for the divine on the inside, rather than from God. This comes very close to the philosophies behind yoga and TM.

Paul's answer is very clear. God's secret is Christ, not a superior "knowledge" or set of new experiences. We cannot save ourselves; salvation must come from outside ourselves. Christ, who is God in the flesh, is our only source of salvation. We are to focus on and follow Him. In other words, when we meditate, it should be on Him, His work, and His words.

Some might say, "But I use yoga to help me relax and alleviate stress – I am not following their philosophy." Relaxation techniques and stress reduction methods can be legitimate for the Christian. Two key questions are: "What is the goal?" and "Am I opening up myself to something that could move me away from Christ?" If the goal is to relax/reduce stress in order to better serve Christ, and I am not dabbling with a philosophy that moves me away from Him, that could be legitimate. Otherwise, we may be subtly swayed to move in directions that seem innocent, but could have very negative consequences.

Meditation can be legitimate, if we meditate on God and His Word. It is the "filling" of our minds with the goal to know God better and equip ourselves for His work. Clearing or "emptying" our minds to receive new experiences, find "enlightenment" or achieve a "higher form of consciousness" is not taught in Scripture (in fact, just the contrary) and should not be the goal of the Christian. This kind of philosophy and meditation is dangerous for the Christian.

Hypnosis

Earlier in this chapter I discussed how meditation in and of itself is basically neutral; it is the type and goal of meditation that can make it legitimate or not for the Christian. The same can be said for hypnosis. While it seems like one person has control of another, or it seems like a "spell" is cast, it is not the case. If we only look at what it "seems" to be, it is no wonder that Christians denounce it as a type of sorcery, a dabbling with the demonic, or some sort of mind control. It is none of the above.

While hypnosis does involve a "trance" state, it is no different than the "trance" I sometimes see in my students during a long lecture, or what we experience driving down the road when we cannot remember if we went through a town or not (and we obviously did!). We all have "zoned out" while still engaging in certain activities, and it does not mean another person or a demon has control of us.

If we watch a hypnotist on stage or in a counseling session, it appears that the hypnotist has "power" over the subject. Again, this is not the case. The power is not in the hypnotist – it resides with the subject ho is open to suggestion.[217] It is merely suggesting things to suggestible people who are in a relaxed state. Hypnosis cannot force people to act against their will – otherwise, the government would be using it on us quite often!

Hypnosis has been used to uncover forgotten memories, but this can be dangerous. Memory is quite susceptible to being altered by suggestions from others. People claim to find "past lives" or report being

---

[217] K.S. Bowers. "Hypnosis," *Personality and behavioral disorders* (New York: Wiley, 1984).

abducted by aliens while under hypnosis, with no evidence to support such claims.

Hypnosis is simply a tool. "Posthypnotic suggestions have helped alleviate headaches, asthma, and stress related skin disorders."[218] Hypnosis can alleviate pain. Myers (2008) states, "And nearly 10 percent of us can become so deeply hypnotized that even major surgery can be performed without anesthetic."[219] How does this happen? As with dissociation, there appears to be a split between levels of consciousness. As William James (1890) said, "The total possible consciousness may be split into parts which co-exist but mutually ignore each other."[220]

In the previous chapter, I discussed how the unconscious is a reality using logic alone, and the fact that the Bible deals with the notion of unconscious sin. Freud and others were correct in their assumption of an unconscious realm, and hypnosis may be a tool to tap into this realm. While the Bible does address the unconscious, does it have anything to say about hypnosis?

Some have said that Adam was "hypnotized" in Gen. 2:21-22 when God caused him to go into a "deep sleep" and a rib was removed (surgery!) to make Eve. In Acts 10:9-10, Peter "fell into a trance" and then had a vision that was used by God to give the gospel to Gentiles. While I would not say that these verses refer to "hypnotism" as we think of it, it does tell us something about how the mind can work.

If hypnosis is simply a tool, the real question to ask is, "How is the tool being used?" If it is used to help deal with negative thinking, improper emotional reactions, and damaging behavior, could it be a good thing? If it is used to move people away from God, then of course it is illegitimate. I believe as a tool, hypnosis is neutral, but as a tool, it can be used for good or for evil. As I said with meditation, the goal is the key. In meditation, if we focus and concentrate on the right things, it is legitimate. Could hypnosis be used to focus and concentrate on those things as well? Since there is an unconscious realm, could this be a tool that gives aid to our conscious minds?

---

[218] D.G. Myers, Exploring psychology 7th ed. (New York: Worth, 2008). p. 201.
[219] Myers, Exploring psychology, p. 201.
[220] William James, The principles of psychology, (London: Macmillan, 1890), p. 206.

CHAPTER 8

SELF-CONCEPT/SELF-ESTEEM/BIBLICAL DIGNITY

A Proper View of Self

What is the proper way to view ourselves? Is self-esteem a biblical concept? Shouldn't we be "others-centered" and not think about ourselves? Is that possible? Is any type of self-focus legitimate? These are important questions for us to ponder.

Many Christians work hard to attain "others-centeredness" -- rightly striving to attain something that God has asked us to embrace. Yet some who "pronounce" and advertise their others-centeredness are the very ones who miss the mark the most. And in their attempts to hit that goal, they demonstrate a proud focus on themselves and an uncanny selfishness that still categorizes their behavior.

There is a way to have a proper view of self. But could it be that "ME" has to be properly taken care of so that "ME" gets out of the way and I am able to focus on "YOU"? If one doesn't do that, he will probably continue to be selfish and may not even be aware of his defective thinking and actions. It is our goal to be others-centered. But maybe there needs to be a proper sense of self for us to do that.

In dealing with the subject of "self-esteem," Christians tend to fall into one of two extremes: **1)** "**You've got to "love" yourself** (before you can love God or others) or **2)** "**You've got to "reject" yourself** (a way to interpret the passages that speak of "denying" the self).

Love Yourself

People in the first group say that you need to "love" yourself before you can "love" God and others. "If you don't love yourself, you can't love them." They will often quote Matthew 22:37 and 39 which say, "Love the Lord your God with all your heart and with all your soul and with all your mind (v. 37) . . . And . . . Love your neighbor as yourself" (v. 39). So it follows, they say, that if you don't love yourself, there is no way you can love God and/or your neighbor.

The author of this text would disagree with that interpretation of Matthew 22 for the following reason: Matthew 22 conveys love of "yourself" as *standard* -- "Love your neighbor as you ALREADY love yourself." It is not a command to love yourself. It is a standard.

How do we already love ourselves? When we're tired, we rest. When we're hungry, we eat. When we have a headache, we take a pain reliever. If we are choosing a seat in an auditorium, we look for one by the aisle, or where there is a good view, or where there is foot room, or whatever our preference. When it's sunny, we go outside. When it's cold, we put on a coat. We naturally gravitate toward things that help us feel good or comfortable and away from things that make us feel bad or are less desirable. In fact, that is why we accepted Christ. We realized that there was something there that we wanted. We naturally look after ourselves *with no conditions.* We are "self"-ish[221] by nature.

That "selfishness" can be a good thing. We avoid putting our hand in the flame because it hurts. That avoidance of pain and "looking after oneself" helps keep our body protected. God promises rewards for living for Him. We like rewards. God created us to "want" good things. (We are also like Him in that way. He wants good things. He wants a relationship with us. He wants us to choose Him in order to have a perfect relationship with Him. He wants us to go His way and to avoid sin. He wants to give us the place that He has prepared for us.)

So we naturally "love" ourselves and we naturally seek good things for ourselves. Consequently, when Christ instructed us to love our neighbors as ourselves (Matt. 22:39), it is this author's belief that He was saying, "Here's the way to love others -- the way you already love you." So if we already "love" ourselves (look after our own good or comfort) then what is it that hinders our ability to love others well? The problem seems to stem from our understanding and belief about how we are already unconditionally and individually loved by God.

In many places in the Bible (such as 1 John 4:19) it says, "We love because He first loved us." It doesn't say, "We love because **WE** first loved us." It seems clear that it is a misinterpretation to say that we must love ourselves. God has never asked us to do that. It is something we already do.

---

[221] Hyphenated to draw distinction from negative form of selfishness.

Deny Yourself

The other extreme, which is especially common among those who oppose the "self-esteemers" and who criticize people who believe in "self-esteem,"[222] is to say, "All self-esteem is anthropocentric, man-centered, and entirely anti-biblical." They say that "esteeming" oneself contradicts biblical teachings. "The Bible says to DENY YOURSELF! (Mark 8:34). You are to 'PUT YOURSELF DOWN,' take up your cross, and follow Him."

If you find yourself in that category, then think about what you are going to have for dinner tonight. Is it something that you like? How much will you indulge your eating pleasure? Shouldn't you be eating only just enough food to keep you alive? And maybe you shouldn't eat anything that you really like, because if you do, you are thinking of yourself.

Sometimes those who disavow "self-esteem" are people with plump bellies who are on their way to dinner in hopes of a good steak. But if you truly believe that we should have NO self-focus, then something that seems contradictory is going on. Somewhere in there you are not denying yourself. Somewhere in there you are saying, "This 'self-indulgence' is okay."

Though some Christians oppose "self-esteem" who sincerely desire to please God, they may be enlightened to find that there is another, probably better, interpretation of Mark 8:34. There is another way of understanding what it means to have a proper self-focus.

---

[222] Author's note: I don't like the term "self-esteem," but I can live with it, as long as it is defined correctly.

Better Interpretation of "Self-Denial" Verses

The Bible does teach denial of the self. So what does that mean? Does it mean, "Don't get a good steak," "Don't sleep in a comfortable bed"? No, it doesn't mean that.

What does it mean to deny yourself? It means "Don't let yourself get in the way!" "Don't make yourself god." "Don't make YOU the most important thing in the world."

Following God and loving Him and others is more important than getting what we want. We are still going to take care of ourselves. And we are still going to enjoy pleasurable things (and thank God for them). But when the choice exists to help others and serve God, we will work to put our unnecessary pleasures aside to serve others -- to place others' needs first, to be there if they need us.

We can please God by taking care of ourselves both physically and spiritually. Engaging in doing things that help nourish and refresh ourselves can help us be better able to do God's work. Psalm 1 talks about a righteous "blessed" man when it says, "He is like a tree planted by the streams of water, which yields its fruit in season and whose leaf does not wither."

What is it that the tree is doing? It's staying by the river to get nourishment so it can produce fruit (for others to eat) and shade and limbs for the birds. Our goal should be to be others-centered, while we are getting what we need. There's a healthy form of "self-ishness." Just like feeding ourselves physically, we need to take care of ourselves spiritually/psychologically, so that we can love well.

If we let ourselves "dry up," we are not going to be much good to the birds and our fruit isn't going to be very tasty or healthy -- if we are able to produce fruit at all. We can't "give" what we don't have to give. We can't be as effective for God if we don't take care of ourselves. So we want to stay close to the water – both physically and spiritually/psychologically. That's good, "healthy selfishness."

We can still enjoy the pleasures that God gives us. King David was blessed with many riches, yet they weren't his god. He had plenty to eat and he probably dined well. He probably enjoyed good music. (We know he played the harp – 1 Samuel 16.) We can assume that he dressed well since he was king. And he enjoyed the abundance that God had given him (just as others did, such as Job, Esther, Jacob, and other godly people mentioned in the Bible). Yet those things did not become his gods. His most important duty was to do God's will. That was made evident in the Psalms and in the way he lived his life, even when he dealt with his own sin.

So to summarize the two positions: The improper "love yourself" position falls off on one side saying, "**It's all about me.** I've got to learn how to "love" myself and until I get me fixed up, I can't help you." That's going TOO FAR. The improper "deny yourself" position says, "**I'm never going to think about me.**" That's going too FAR the other way! There is a healthy balance. We need to "love ourselves" properly and "deny ourselves" properly. We need to take care of ourselves appropriately so that we can love God and love others in the best manner possible, yet deny ourselves when others need our attention. Again, finding that **balance is the key.**

Four Helpful Concepts

The following are four concepts that are helpful when dealing with the topic of self-esteem or what the author prefers to label "biblical dignity." The concepts are: **1) Coping Skills, 2) Dignity, 3) Depravity, and 4) Dependency.**

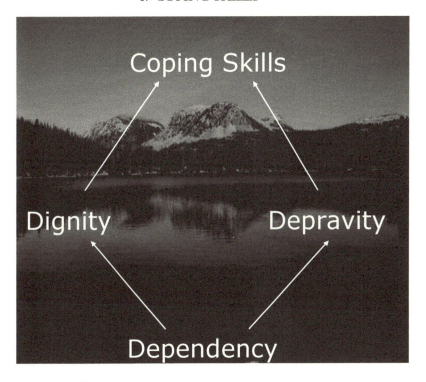

As can be seen on the chart, "Coping Skills" are ABOVE the water line while Dignity, Depravity, and Dependency are BELOW the water line. "Coping Skills" refer to the techniques that are often employed by counselors to help raise self-esteem in clients. The problem is that many times when a conversation about building someone's self-esteem takes place, the discussion involves helping the client develop better coping skills. The difficulty there is that coping skills are ABOVE the water line.[223] There are a number of people who would rather talk about coping skills -- which they say promote a high "self-esteem" -- than discuss the ideas of Dignity, Depravity, and Dependency. That's part of the problem with the "self-esteem movement." Techniques are often utilized that have

---

[223] Picture of Mirror Lake below Bald Mountain in Wyoming. Public domain. Talbot Hauffe / Wyoming Department of Transportation http://library.byways.org/assets/75682, accessed 1.11.11. Chart designed by Thomas J. Edgington, Ph.D.

not been built on a solid foundation.

"Self-esteem" was more of a "hot" topic in the 1990s than today; but because there are still people who ask, "What do you think about the whole 'self-esteem' topic?" this chapter addresses some of the issues that have accompanied the techniques associated with the movement. The following is a list of some coping skills, many of which have been promoted by the Self-Esteem Movement and an explanation as to why they fall short.

1) Love Yourself. The idea here has to do with an emotional, relational "feeling." The problem with this technique or skill is that you can't do it to yourself. Self-care, yes, you can do that; you can make yourself comfortable and free from physical pain. But to really *feel* love for yourself the way you want to be loved by another person, no, you can't love yourself that way. That kind of love HAS TO come from the outside.

We love because "HE first loved us" (1 John 4:19). When we get that love from the outside, THEN we are capable of loving. If we don't have it, we can't give it to ourselves! We were created to need relational love.

In the 1990s, Al Franken's *Saturday Night Live* character, Stuart Smalley, used to look into a mirror and say, "I'm good enough, I'm smart enough, and, doggonit, people like me!" [225] But techniques like that -- which were intended to make us feel better about ourselves -- haven't worked. "Loving yourself" falls short because love is a relational term. You can't do it in a way that truly satisfies.

2) Emphasize the Positives. "Hey! Let's focus on what's positive about you." "What is good about you?" Emphasizing positives can be a helpful coping skill.

In and of itself, this is not a BAD technique and could align itself with Paul's teaching in Philippians 4 for us to think on good things. In general, coping skills are not BAD techniques, EXCEPT when they are exclusive. If we are only talking about building someone's self-esteem by methods that do not take into account how God created us, sin, and what He does for us, then we are going to miss the most important elements that will help us feel truly fulfilled.

---

[225] "Daily Affirmations with Stuart Smalley," SNL Transcripts, from Sept 28, 1991, http://snltranscripts.jt.org/91/91asmalley.phtml and http://snlarc.jt.org/skit.php?i=96 accessed 1/31/10.

3) Correct Self-Talk. What about changing the way we talk to ourselves? If you were able to change those BAD messages you give yourself, would that change the way you feel about yourself? If you stopped telling yourself, "Nobody likes me," and replaced that message with, "I am cared about by others," or "It doesn't matter if others don't like me because God loves me," would that help? Or if you changed, "I'm no good," to "I have value," or "I have gifts," could that help fulfill your needs?

Telling yourself the right kinds of messages can be helpful. We should all develop good "self-talk" based on the things we know and believe. Again, it's biblical to think on good things – Phil. 4. But if exclusive, those "techniques" are going to fall short.

4) "Self-Affirmation" – Affirm Yourself. This is similar to "Correct Self-talk" except that this is telling yourself specific good things about you. Changing, "I'm bad," to "I've done some good things today," or "I'm dumb," to "I've got some smarts," or "I only lost two pounds/I'm fat!" to "Wow, I lost two pounds!/I'm taking better care of myself," can be helpful. Thinking differently about things that you don't like about yourself can be a good technique – but again, not independently. Taking it too far (as with the previous three skills) without the proper foundation can lead to pride – as noted later in this chapter.

5) Improve Your Social Skills. Counselors use this avenue to help their clients adapt better to their world. They may say, "You've got to learn to look into people's eyes when you talk to them. Shake their hand. Use their name. Act confident." Learning better social skills can help you feel better about yourself, and when your relationships improve, you will probably feel better all around. There is some truth to that, but it falls short.

6) Assertiveness. This method promotes asking for what you want and not backing down when your honesty would be helpful. "Be assertive." "Don't be aggressive, but be assertive." "Don't be passive. Get out there and don't be afraid to give your opinion and/or state your needs."

Sometimes assertiveness training can promote self-centeredness when the implementer ignores others' needs and when his implementation is not built on a foundation of his own primary needs having been met. Again, there is a biblical form of assertiveness. There is a biblical confidence that we ought to have (Isaiah 6:8, 2 Cor. 5:6). This isn't it.

7) Make Better Choices. "Choose better friends." "Go back to school." "Change your career." "Do what you want to do! Quit doing what other people tell you to do. Do what YOU want to do!" There is some value to those statements. But again, you've got the same problem if they are techniques that aren't built on a foundation of understanding what God has given. Just making "better choices" will not ultimately satisfy.

All of the seven previously stated ideas, when implemented, only deal with areas "above" the "water line." They are all good ideas and we can still practice them, but they will only be truly helpful with the proper understanding of what is beneath. If people just change their "skills," they could possibly feel a bit better about themselves, but for some of the wrong reasons. The "skills" will "work" on some level. But the coping skills are basically attempts to feel better apart from God, so there will still exist a sense of neediness or incompleteness that hasn't been met or filled.

So to summarize, most of the time when people talk about building self-esteem, they are talking about developing better coping skills – ONLY. They are not dealing with some of the deeper realities that need to be dealt with. Ideas like, "Let's build self-esteem in our kids," or "Let's have a high self-esteem," are ideas that seem to be popular among many; but if we try to promote "self-esteem" without laying a proper foundation for that topic, then we bypass three very important doctrines. If you don't understand those doctrines, then you'll miss the most important foundational pieces.

The following discussion will deal with those foundational principles "below the water line." In order to understand proper "self-esteem" from a biblical perspective, three principles are important to look at -- Dignity, Depravity, and Dependency.

Below the Water Line -- 3-D's Dignity, Depravity, Dependency

2. BIBLICAL DIGNITY

God says we have intrinsic dignity. In previous chapters, we established that we were created in the image and likeness of God (Gen. 1:26). When marveling over the creation of man in Psalm 8:5-6, the Bible says: "You made him a little lower than the heavenly beings and crowned him with glory and honor. You made him ruler over the works of your hands; you put everything under his feet." God created us to rule over the earth. He crowned us with glory and honor. So we HAVE intrinsic dignity.

It is not the kind, necessarily, where we go around saying, "Wow, am I great!" because all of us have the same thing -- we are all image-bearers; nevertheless, it sets us apart from the other created beings. Unfortunately, there is something that gets in the way of that dignity -- our depravity -- which is the next "D" we will deal with.

Read Matthew 6:26. "Look at the birds of the air; they do not sew, or reap, or store away in barns, and yet your heavenly Father feeds them. Are you not much more valuable than they?" And the NASB says, "Are you not worth much more than they?" The Bible talks about our worth and value! And many other verses allude to that value (1 Cor. 6:20, 7:23; Rom. 8:15; Gal. 4:6, etc.). *Dignity is a value assigned to us by God.*

Our dignity is made even more evident after we become Christians because we are "children of God" (1 John 3:1). And the Bible says that we have a unique importance and worth because of that. God values us.

But we cannot have dignity without a proper sense of dependency. We can't have a dignity apart from God. So we have got to start with Him and look at ourselves the way God looks at us.

How does God look at us? He loves us. We have worth and value to Him. Why? Because He says we do. We are useful to His purposes. If we look at ourselves the way God does and not how other people have looked at us, we can have a godly sense of confidence that propels us to move out into our world.

Dignity and self-esteem without God move us into the area of pride. When we try to have "self-esteem" without God, we are saying, "I am 'great'" in and of myself, and I don't need God. That is a dangerous place to be. Godless "dignity" is pride. But when we recognize God as our creator and father, we enjoy an unconditional love and value and an intrinsic "dignity" that we can accept in humility because of what He has done for us.

3. DEPRAVITY

That leads us to the next "D" regarding why He died for us. It was because of our depravity. You are not as BAD as you can be, but certainly as BAD OFF as you can be (Jer. 17:9; Rom. 1:18-32; Rom. 5:12; Eph. 2:1; Ps. 51:5; Isa. 64:6). (We talked about this in previous chapters.) Without Christ, in the presence of God we are in trouble. No matter how much dignity we have, we are still in trouble. We can't just fall back on our dignity and say that is enough. Our depravity is so destructive that it overshadows our dignity.

Most "self-esteemers" want to bypass the three principles (dignity, depravity, and dependency) because they say that if you look at such things as depravity, you are going to feel worse about yourself. That may be true. But is that necessarily a bad thing?

When you feel bad about yourself, it can move you to a good place because you are going to take care of some things that are wrong with you. It is like looking in the mirror.

You might have had that experience this morning. You looked in the mirror and said to yourself, "This does not look good!"

Now, you could have just berated yourself and said, "I am so ugly that I'm just going to hate myself for the rest of the day!" That would have been a possible choice.

Or you could have said, "Oh! That is ugly! I want to do something about it," and proceeded to shower, shave, fix your hair, apply makeup, etc. Then you would have looked much better.

That is really what God is trying to do with us. God is saying, "I want to put a spotlight on your sin so you'll do something about it. . .make yourself better in the right way -- by accepting Me and following Me."

And so it is true that you are probably going to feel worse about yourself if you look at your sin. But you don't have to stop there and criticize yourself – labeling yourself a "worthless worm." You can take note of the deficiencies and think, "What do I need to do to make this better?" and/or "What do I need to do to grow?" Or if you don't know

Christ you can ask yourself, "What do I need to do, to know Him?" If we move to self-contempt and stay there, we are simply moving to another form of sin.

Depravity blocks us from our dignity. Depravity gets in the way. We can't go around proclaiming, "Hey! I'm an image-bearer! I feel great about myself! I don't have any problems!" because we have deep problems! Given our depravity, we deserve Hell. So depravity is a HUGE problem that must be incorporated into one's view of self-esteem; otherwise, dignity by itself isn't going to be sufficient.

How is self-contempt another form of sin? One thing that self-contempt does is it gives a person a measure of control. If you could just hate yourself, it does a couple of things.

Number 1 -- Because you are in control of it, you don't have to really face your shame. In your self-contempt, you feel as though you have some control over your wretched condition. You don't have to DO anything about it except "beat yourself up." It tells everybody, "Look, my standards are a lot higher than this and I should be better than this. I'm really a good person and my 'beating myself up' confirms that." You can stay in your wretched condition --espousing good goals -- so you don't really have to deal with your sin.

Number 2 -- It becomes a way of getting relationship. It gets people to reassure you, to feel sorry for you, to tell you positive things in order to try to get you out of your self-contempt.

God says, "That's not the right way of handling self-contempt. It's not the right way of handling what's inside of you." The right way of handling it is: confession, repentance, accepting what He's done and humbly saying, "Yes, I deserve Hell. Thank you that you are giving me Heaven. Now, I want to live my life to please you."

So we have got to understand dignity and depravity correctly to have a proper sense of self-esteem. If we don't deal with our depravity, our dignity means very little.

In order to deal with our depravity, God sent Jesus so that we could be justified and sanctified, in spite of our sin. Christ redeemed us, which is even better than our being perfect.

Why is it better to be saved -- to be justified and sanctified -- than to be perfect? Well, why would God allow sin to come into the world? What else does sin (along with redemption) do? Would we have known grace?

Would we have known mercy? Would we have known unconditional love? Would we have known many of the attributes of God if we had been perfect? -- No. There is no need for grace. There is no need for mercy. There is no need for unconditional love.

So part of the reason why God allowed sin to come in was to show us the God of grace, and the God of mercy, and the God of kindness, and the God who is long-suffering, and the God of unconditional love, that He is. We wouldn't have known that without sin. That is not saying that God WANTED sin, but He certainly uses it to show Himself in a way that we would not have known Him otherwise. That is why redemption is better than perfection. We understand God in a way that we couldn't have, had we been perfect.

It is freeing and calming to know that we don't have to be perfect or reach a certain standard to be accepted by God. Sure, we can want that and work toward that. There is something good about striving for the ideal. But to entertain the idea that, "Somehow if I become perfect, then everything is going to be great," is entertaining a fantasy. Number one, we can't do it, and number two, that is not what God has in mind.

He wants us to understand, "You are a mess! You deserve Hell. But I have taken care of that. It's all done. You're in. Not only that, you are sealed. I've got a place for you. It's guaranteed." He wants us to know that because of Christ – a perfect savior – we are declared to be perfect, but in and of ourselves, we cannot make ourselves perfect.

When we get a hold of that, then we can realize how amazing His grace is, and that transforms us. That is what transformation is all about. That is what spurs us to grow -- much more than, "Wow, I did that perfectly! That feels really good." It is okay to do some things well sometimes and feel good about that. But what really causes us to grow is understanding the depth of our depravity and then realizing who God is and what He has done for us.

4. DEPENDENCY

Which leads us to the final "D" – Dependency. If we are perfect, then we are not dependent. At least we wouldn't have that feeling of, "Yeah, I can pretty well handle life because I'm perfect and I don't really need God." So maybe God allowed sin to come into the world for us to realize our dependency. Without depending on God to get us out of the "mess" (our depravity), we are in big trouble! We need God. We need His love. We need His meaning and purpose to life. We need His salvation. We need Him for everything that is important in life. We are "dependent" on Him.

Dependency is the state we are in as we relate to our creator. We've got to have that as the underpinning of both dignity and depravity. Recalling the chart with the water line, "dependency" was at the base. You HAVE TO start there. Without a proper sense of dependency, you cannot get to a proper sense of dignity, depravity, or skills to cope with life. Dependency must be the foundation of everything pertaining to self-concept and self-esteem.

So pulling it all together, read Isaiah 6, verses 1 through 8.

> In the year that King Uzziah died, I saw the Lord seated on a throne, high and exalted, and the train of his robe filled the temple. Above him were seraphs, each with six wings: With two wings they covered their faces, with two they covered their feet, and with two they were flying. And they were calling to one another: "Holy, holy, holy is the Lord Almighty; the whole earth is full of his glory." At the sound of their voices the door-posts and thresholds shook and the temple was filled with smoke. "Woe to me!" I cried. "I am ruined! For I am a man of unclean lips, and I live among a people of unclean lips, and my eyes have seen the King, the Lord Almighty." Then one of the seraphs flew to me with a live coal in his hand, which he had taken with tongs from the altar. With it he touched my mouth and said, "See, this has touched your lips; and your guilt is taken away and your sin atoned for." Then I heard the voice of the Lord saying, "Whom shall I send? And who will go for us?" And I said, "Here am I. Send me!"

That is probably the best passage that can be found to show how godly confidence is built. First of all, we have to -- in dependence -- go to God, realizing that He is God and we are not. In the first few verses, you will notice God's holiness is shaking up the place. Even Hollywood would have trouble demonstrating what it would be like to be in the presence of God, but these verses are trying to tell us what it is like. If we were actually in the presence of God, we would probably be awestruck. We would feel that utterly deficient comparison that Isaiah wrote about expressing: "You are perfect. We are not." We would be falling on our faces. Even the angels were covering their faces. It was too much for them to look directly at God. They exclaimed, "Holy, Holy, Holy. You are God."

And when Isaiah looked over the entire scene and took in the majesty and holiness of God, he immediately said, "Woe to me!" When we are in the presence of God's holiness, we realize how unclean we are. We realize how sinful we are.

Peter also had an experience like that. Mark 5:8 tells of Peter falling to his face upon realizing that he was in the presence of God. He proclaimed his unworthiness to be in Christ's presence as he said, "Go away from me, Lord; I am a sinful man."

There is something good about realizing who man is and how undeserving he is to be in the presence of the almighty God. That is not self-contempt. That is humility.

"Woe to me," Isaiah cried. "I am ruined!" [I am a mess!] "I am a man of unclean lips." [I'm sinful. I have problems.]   And then he evaluates the rest of his world and notices that they aren't much better either: "I live among a people of unclean lips" (v. 6:5). Isaiah is saying, "We are all a mess!"

Isaiah says, "And my eyes have seen the king. . . ." Then, one of the seraphs flew to him with a live coal from the altar. What is that supposed to symbolize? Why would the seraph take a live coal from the altar?

It is burning. It symbolizes redemption. It is saying, "I want to SAVE you."

The altar was where sacrifices were taken. Christ is now THE sacrifice. We don't have to take animals to sacrifice on the altar anymore. But at the time that Isaiah wrote this, the altar was what made a person "right" before God.

God was telling Isaiah, "I'm going to take a live coal and put it to your unclean lips" – indicating that He is going to redeem him, yet with a warning, "It is going to be painful." Redemption is painful and, yet, ultimately satisfying.

When we accept Christ's sacrifice for us and are "saved," we realize the extent of our sinfulness. We realize how bad we are. It is a painful process.

But it is only as we are fallen and realize, "It's only you, God, and what you offer to me that can save me," that God reaches down and lifts up our chin. It is when we are saying, "I am going through this painful process and I realize how unclean my lips are," that God says to us, "It's all taken care of. You are in. You don't have to do anything else. You are saved. You are sanctified. You are glorified. I've got a place waiting for you."

That is why Isaiah gave the response that He did to the Lord's questions. "The Lord said, 'Who shall I send? Who will go for us?'" And what was Isaiah's response? "Here I am. Send me!"

Redemption is the answer to depravity: "I am fallen, but I am redeemed and I can do something for you that matters."

Why didn't Isaiah say, "Not me! I'm a worthless worm." He had already gone through that. But now that he has been redeemed, look at his response: "Send me. I'll go for you."

When the topic of shame is approached, some wonder if and when it is appropriate to feel shame and when it is long enough to stay in that state of proclaiming utter wretchedness. There is a point when we need to be ready to move on. We need to feel our shame, acknowledge our unworthiness, and then cease to dwell there anymore. Because we have God as our support, we can move out in confidence to serve Him.

It takes confidence to move out. Yet, Isaiah's response was based on a proper sense of dignity, depravity, and dependency. He could feel confident because He had the almighty God as his foundation, as his motivation and inspiration. He was saying, "Given what you've done for me, I want to do some things for you."

The Answer to "Self-Esteem"/Biblical Dignity

That is the answer to building appropriate "self-esteem" (biblical dignity). Once we understand how He made us – that he has given us **dignity**, that our **depravity** has been dealt with, and that we need Him and He is there for us -- **dependency**, we can have a godly sense of confidence that propels us to want to serve. At that point, changing our "coping skills" can be helpful.

Godless self-esteem that makes us independent from God does not lead to lasting peace. The existentialists and the humanists declare that man is "god." When people are taught godless self-esteem, they are taught the error that man can make life work well by himself. The truth is that man does not feel a sense of total peace apart from God. He is still striving to find something that will deeply satisfy. Feeling total contentment apart from God is a fallacy! Ultimately, though one can feel "good" about making appropriate behavioral changes, those changes cannot take away man's neediness. The changes still lead to emptiness.

Some people, after alcohol rehab or AA meetings, are sober all the way to Hell. Getting sober is a good thing, but it doesn't get to eternal matters. We want people to get off of the alcohol. But there is more to it than that. There is more to eternal peace than feeling good about one's accomplishments, feeling good that one is not addicted anymore, feeling that one has a personal sense of power.

Those can be good -- if they are viewed in the proper sense of dependency. When we understand how God has made us and what He has done for us, we can feel good (and a deeper/richer sort of "good") in our dependency on the Almighty.

When building on the three D's, moving out and considering helpful options for our lives is now appropriate. The coping skills can be useful now: "I want to go back to school." "I want to get a new job." "I want to learn social skills." "I want to look people in the eye." "I want to do those things that are going to make me better." Nothing is wrong with learning those skills and applying those techniques. We can feel good about those things. And with a proper understanding of dignity, depravity, and dependency, we can look at all the aspects of our lives and make changes for the better. They are external changes that come out of depth -- out of good internal work. When we build the proper foundation, we are equipped to move out as God's representatives in a sinful world.

SCRIPTURAL INDEX ACCORDING TO
PAGE NUMBER

69	James 1:8; Dan. 4:28-33
70	John 8:44
73	Ps. 111:2; Gen. 1:28
74	Phil. 2:10
76	Prov. 23:7
85	James 2:1-4
89	Prov. 22:2; Prov. 29:13; Matt. 5:45
90	Matt. 5:45; Ps. 14:1; 1 Cor. 15:33
91	Titus 1:12, 13
92	Heb. 5:14; Phil. 1:9-10
93	2 Pet. 1:3; Gen. 1:28
98	1 Sam. 16:1-7
99	1 Sam. 17:28
101	1 Sam. 13:14; Acts 13:22
102	Matt. 6:5, 6:7
103	John 13:35
104	Matt. 23, 23:27; 23:25; 23:23; Luke 18:10-14; Matt. 23:4; Matt. 16:5
107	John 4:24; Acts 7:55, 56
108	John 10:36; Mark 10:33; Job 1:6
109	Rev. 6:9; Heb. 12:23; John 4:24
110	2 Cor. 5:2, 3; 2 Cor. 5:4; Luke 23:46: James 2:26
115	1 Cor. 6:19; Acts 7:55, 56
116	Rom. 8:23; 1 Cor. 15:42-44
118	Matt. 10:28; 1 Cor. 6:18
119	John 20:27; Gen. 18-19; Gen 18:22
120	Gen. 18, 19; Acts 7:55-56; Matt. 10:28
121	Job 1:6; Job 1:7; Gen. 1: 26, 27; Gen. 18-19; 5:1; 9:6; 1 Cor. 11:7; James 3:9

122	2 Cor. 5:8
123	1 Sam. 28:1-20; Luke 16:19-31; Luke 23:46; Matt. 10:28, 26:41; Phil. 1:24; 2 Cor. 5:9, 7:1; James 2:26
124	Luke 16:19-31; Luke 23:46, Matt. 10:28, 26:41; 2 Cor. 5:9, 7:1; Phil. 1:24; James 2:26
125	Matt. 10:28; 1 Cor. 7:34
126	Heb. 12:23; Rev. 6:9
127	1 Thes. 5:23; Mark 12:30; Matt. 22:37; Deut. 6:5
128	1 John 3:17; Lam. 1:20, 2:11
129	Gen. 17:14; Num. 31:28, Acts 2:43, 3:23
130	Jer. 6:8; 9:9
131	Gen. 2:7; Exod. 4:19; Lev. 17:11; 1 Sam. 2:33; Prov. 23:7; Eph. 6:6
132	Eph. 6:6; Num. 19:13; Lev. 21:11; Num. 6:6; Hag. 2:13
133	Matt. 10:28; Rev. 6:9; Ps. 63
134	Rev. 13:15
135	Exod. 28:3; Gen. 41:8
136	Num. 16:22, Ps. 51:10; 1 Cor. 7: 34; Heb. 12:23; 1 Cor. 15:44
137	Heb. 4:12; 1 Thes. 5:23; Matt. 22:37
143	Heb. 9:27
144	Gen. 1:1; Zech. 12:1; Isa. 57:16; Heb. 12:9; Jer. 1:5
145	Heb. 12:9; Ps. 139:13-16
146	Ps. 139:15; Jer. 1:5; Ps. 139:13-16;
147	Gen. 2:2; Exod. 20:11;
148	1 Cor. 6:18; Ps. 51:5
149	Eph. 2:3; Rom. 5; Rom. 5:12
150	Gen. 18; Gen. 5:3; John 1:13
151	Acts 17:26
152	Luke 2:40
153	Ps. 51:5; Eph. 2:3

155   Matt. 19:14; Luke 18:16; 2 Sam. 12:23, Gen. 9:6

158   Gen. 1:26, 27, 5:1, 9:6; 1 Cor. 11:7; James 3:9

160   Gen: 3:8

161   Gen. 9

162   Acts 7:56; John 3:35; 15:10; Matt. 10:40; John 16:5, 17:3, 17:18;

163   John 14:16; 17:1-26, John 17:4; John 17; John 16:7; John 16:14;
       Col. 3:5

164   Rom. 6:6; Isa. 64:6; Col. 3:5

166   Rom. 7:23

167   Rom. 6:6; Eph. 4:22-24; Col. 3:9-10

170   Prov. 20:12; Ps. 94:9; Ps. 115:3-8; Deut. 34:7; Rev. 1:7;
       Matt. 6:22,23; 7:3-5; 13:16; Rev. 3:18; John 3:3; Ps. 119:105;
       Mark 8:22-24; 10:46-52; John 9:2-3; John 9:2-7

171   Acts 9:8-18; 2 Cor. 5:7; Ex. 30:38; Ps. 45:8; John 12:3; Gen. 8:21;
       Lev. 8:21; Lev. 26:31; Ps. 141:2; Phil. 4:18; Isa. 3:24; 2 Cor. 2:15;
       Matt. 5:13; Col. 4:6; Ps. 119:103; Matt. 16:28; Heb. 2:9;
       Prov. 24:13; Col. 2:21; Ps. 34:8; Matt. 9:21,29-30; Mark 5:41;
       10:13-16; 1 Cor. 7:1-5

172   1 John 1:1-4; Luke 24:39; Isa. 45:23; Rom. 14:11; Phil. 2:10;
       Matt. 6:23-24; John 3:3; Titus 1:15; John 6:44; Eph. 1:18;
       John 8:12; Jer. 33:3; Isa. 55:8-9; Phil. 1:9-10; Heb. 5:14

173   Luke 16:19-31; Deut. 18:9-11; 29:29

176   Rom. 3:20; 1 Pet. 2:19; Prov. 10:7; Matt. 26:13; 1 Thes. 3:6

177   John 12:40; 2 Cor. 4:4; 1 John 2:11; Matt. 7:1-6; Ps. 26:4;
       Ps. 44:21; 90:8;

178   Rom. 2:16; 1 Cor. 14:25; Lev. 4:1-5:13; 5:14-6:7; 4:1-35;
       Num. 15:27ff, 30; Lev. 1:1-17; Num. 35:16-18, 22-23

179   Deut. 19:5-6; 1 Sam. 14:32-34; 26:21; Prov. 5:23; Job 6:24; 19:4

180   Leviticus; Lev. 5:1-4; 16:21; 26:40; Num. 5:6-7; 1 John 1:9

181	Lev. 5:14-6:7; Lev. 5 & 6; 5:14-19; 6:1-7; 5:14-16; 4:1-35; 5:17-19; Lev. 22:2-14
182	5:17-19; 16:16; Num. 15:30-31; Ps. 19:13; Job 11:16; Lev. 5:14-16
183	Lev. 5:17-19; Deut 29:28; 1 Sam. 26:19; Ps. 19:13; Job 1:5; Lev. 6:1-7; Num. 15:27ff; Ps. 19:12-13
184	8-12; Jer. 17:9
185	Ps. 19:13a; 130:3; 1 Chron. 28:9; 1 Cor. 4:5; 1 Sam. 16:7; Matt. 7:21-23; Luke 11:27-54; 18:9-14; 18-30; Phil. 1:15-18; Rev. 3:14-22; Prov. 20:5; Ps. 51:16-19; Matt. 15:16-20
187	1 Kings 3:5; Matt. 1:20-21, 2:21-23; Job 33:14-18
188	Ecc. 5:3; Isa. 29:7-8;
189	Ecc. 5:7
190	Josh. 1:8; Ps. 19:14; Ps. 48:9; 77:12; 104:34; 119:15, 148
192	Gen. 2:21-22; Acts 10:9-10
194	Matt. 22:37, 39
195	Matt. 22:37,39; 1 John 4:19
196	Mark 8:34
197	Ps. 1; 1 Sam. 16; Job; Esther;
198	Psalms
200	1 John 4:19
201	Phil. 4; Isa. 6:8; 2 Cor. 5:6
203	Gen. 1:26; Ps. 8:5-6; Matt. 6:26; 1 Cor. 6:20, 7:23; Rom. 8:15; Gal. 4:6; 1 John 3:1
204	Jer. 17:9; Rom. 1:18-32; Rom. 5:12; Eph. 2:1; Ps. 51:5; Isa. 64:6
207	Isa. 6:1-8
208	Isa.6:8; Mark 5:8; Isa. 6:5
209	Isa. 6:5